W9-BUU-016

"Fascinating and thought-provoking! This book will equip you to be your absolute best in all endeavors."

"A Big Help. By far the most effective approach I have encountered for fully developing your competitive self."

"Quite an eye-opener! A peak performance guide unlike any other out there . . . very motivational."

"Entertaining and highly instructional. Easily applicable, simple to understand . . . sports psychology excellence."

"Teaches in a unique and powerful way. Engaging and skillfully written."

"A Life-Changer! A priceless resource . . . One of those rare works destined to become a classic."

"A straight forward guide. I am thrilled to have stumbled upon this amazing book."

"Jolted me into action. An especially engaging book . . . expert insight."

"I wish I would have read this 20 years ago! This book really surprised me."

"Excellent! Enables a new kind of thinking for achieving one's potential through personal transformation."

"Enlightening, Inspirational and Spellbinding! An especially valuable tool . . . captivating."

"Brilliant Work! Many thanks to the author."

"Mental Training from a Master Practitioner . . . You'll never forget DC's teachings."

"Grips you with an utterly compelling writing style and complete fluidity. Its wisdom will impact you."

"Set the Warrior/Champion free! This book stands apart."

"Gonzalez doesn't hold back any secrets. Refreshing, effective and stimulating . . . rooted in reality."

"All I can say is awesome . . . A wonderful journey."

The Art of Mental Training

A Guide to Performance Excellence

By D.C. Gonzalez
with Alice McVeigh

Inspired by True Events

To the Warrior/Champion within you . . .

Contents

Prelude

I never saw Leo-tai angry, but it was he who had taught me how to use the anger energy should it ever arise—and how to effectively redirect it.

"Rather than lose control," he would tell me, "you must learn how to use the energy. You must become like a smiling assassin, Danielsan, and channel the energy; let it help your resolve. If you lose control to the energy, your opponent will win."

It was the use of this concept that led to the "defeat" of several of my opponents without my even having to fight. Sometimes no words are required, only eye contact. With that alone one is marked out as predator, the other as prey: one the assassin, the other the mark. "It is at this subconscious level of communication," Leo-tai once told me, "that one wins a fight without having to fight . . ."

Just as easily as he slipped into my life, Leo-tai slipped out of it, once he had taught me all that he'd meant to teach me. Despite all my best efforts—and all my resources as a Federal Agent—I could locate no financial trail, no property trail, no address, no family, and no contact point . . . he had gone, leaving nothing behind beyond his teachings, and my memory of that half-smile he used to give me when I managed to surprise him.

The last that I heard of Leo-tai was many, many, years ago, second-hand, from sources that I didn't feel I could trust. Until recently, at an invitation function in New York City, I met an elegant elderly lady, an Irish psychic. Internationally recognized and respected in her field, she had also written several books and was currently on a speaking tour when our paths happened to cross.

"You are a teacher," she said the moment we met, "I sense many students around you."

I smiled, but gave her nothing neither as confirmation nor denial; yet she continued: "I'm getting a very clear message from someone who has crossed over and who wants to tell you something. He says that you were friends not only in this life but also as great warriors in another lifetime. He wants me to let you know that he is with you when you teach."

"Oh, really?" I said, using the tone of a seasoned Federal Agent who doesn't believe a single word an informant is telling him.

"Yes, really," she replied, rather ruffled by my skepticism. "He says his name is Leo-tai."

"Did you say Leo-tai?" I asked a little shaken, taken aback.

"Yes, Leo-tai," she repeated, looking away slightly as if listening or searching for a distant memory. Then she turned back to me with sudden certainty.

"He is a very old soul, you know, a great master of the Far East. But please tell me, how is it that you came to know this teacher and what is it that you teach?"

But I could hardly answer . . . for knowing that my old friend was dead.

A Note From DCGonz

Welcome to *The Art of Mental Training*.

Sports Mental Training has been called the Science of Success. But make no mistake. If you imagine that the lessons here apply only to sports and athletes you'd be wrong. For it's the Everyday Warrior, from all walks of life, and all types of scenarios, that stands to benefit immensely from the knowledge and techniques that lie ahead. No matter what you do, or whatever challenges you face, *The Art of Mental Training* can help take you to another level of performance, achievement, and personal success.

Any time that you arrive to engage, event-energy gets mixed in with whatever is going on inside your head at the time. It's the emotions and feelings that this mixture produces that ultimately end up affecting how well we perform.

If, for example, undesired emotions like nervousness, anger, or fear, happen to surface as a result of this mixture, the Warrior/Champion must have the right knowledge, tools, and techniques at his disposal so that he can use them to ensure that his performance does not suffer.

It's what champions know how to do well—and it's something that everyone can learn how to do. But it's only those who set out to learn and practice performance mental training techniques that gain all the benefits and achieve the highest level of results.

The better your self-belief, internal self-talk, attitude, focus, and mental climate are going into an event, the better your situation will be when the event-energy is pumping through you.

By understanding what to shoot for in terms of the *Ideal Mental Climate,* and having been given the knowledge, tools, and techniques required to achieve it, the Warrior/Champion is able to empower all aspects of his performance.

So just for starters . . . understand this:

Whatever is going on inside your head has everything to do with how well you end up performing.

Chapter 1: The Three Minute Lesson

As the mental-edge trainer for university athletics, it was easy for me to spot which athletes wanted the mental training and which athletes didn't care. This particular kid was one of those who just wasn't interested. While the others were listening and thinking, he yawned and admired his biceps. While the other students raised questions or provoked discussions, he was only concerned with the physical aspects of his sport: wrestling. Only a freshman, he was entering the big leagues now—competing at NCAA level for the first time—but that didn't seem to worry him during our sessions.

When it came to the crunch, however, the pressure proved to be just too much. Just a few minutes before his first match at this level, he rushed over to me, distraught and desperate, and started begging for mental training help on the spot. He'd just learned that he'd drawn the top-seeded wrestler in the tournament, a seasoned senior accustomed to annihilating opponents with comparative ease. As chance would have it, my *unbeliever* was about to learn a valuable lesson.

I looked at him and I couldn't help thinking: what an interesting opportunity. This kid is really scared; he's in a completely disempowered state. Clearly, he's not ready to compete at anywhere near the level of his true potential. A real mental mess stood in front of me asking if I could help him, while in his mind's eye, he was already suffering a humiliating defeat at the hands of his opponent. The kid was very shaken, and we only had a few minutes to turn this thing around. He was up next, and the clock didn't show much time left before the current match would end.

With so little time left, what could we do I wondered?

Right then, I remembered something that Leo-tai had told me. "Danielsan, one should never look where one does not wish to go . . ."

I had an idea. "Are you ready to trust me?" I asked him.

"Whatever you say, coach."

"Right. Then step over here and let's get busy."

A few minutes later, when his name was announced, I walked with him to the edge of the mat. He hadn't taken his focus from his task for a single second. All I'd done was to provide him with the mental technique; he did the rest inside his head.

Let me tell you, when that kid stepped on to the mat he was a force of dominance, confidence, and technique. Within a few minutes, he went from a fearful freshman wrestler heading for a crushing defeat, to an unchained gladiator, a champion who owned the arena. He helped to create one of the most exciting high-scoring, action-packed matches of the tournament. The match went the full distance, and in the end my unbeliever had lost the match by only one point. The crowd couldn't believe their eyes. Their champion had barely survived his first match!

What he did is not difficult: no magic, no hypnosis, no smoke or mirrors. I simply guided him through a process with three simple instructions. I gave him one minute to deal with each instruction, before giving him the next one. In that short time, he was able to change his state completely.

I promise that I will teach you exactly how to do this for yourself a little later in the book—and much more—but first, let's think about what this real-life experience brings to light.

I need you to recall an occasion when you performed at your best—and then remember a time when you were at your worst. Now when you look at those two performances, I want you to be honest with yourself and ask, what made the most difference between the two? Could it have been your mental state that made the most difference?

Most athletes will admit that a big part of the difference was exactly that, and that the performance difference had everything to do with their mental state. In the case of this athlete, the difference between what was promising to be one of his worst performances ever, and what had turned out to be one of his best performances ever, was, after all . . . mostly mental.

And that's the important point: no matter what your game is, or what the challenge is, the difference between great performances and average performances is mostly mental. Once you reach a certain level of skill, it's your mental skills that start making all the difference. The better they are, the better you become—and the better your results will be.

Some professional athletes will tell you that they spend considerable time on mental training. They'll tell you how important it is to read books, practice mental techniques, and become accomplished at using relaxation and imagery because they know from experience how it helps their performance. Champions know that the mental game can teach anyone how to stay focused, goal-oriented, and motivated to succeed, as well as how to better deal with both temporary setbacks and real adversity.

The Mental Warrior understands that time spent on the mental game will pay off with improved performance— sometimes almost instantly. The Warrior/Champion learns to use techniques that help him get out of his own way, so he can reach the next possible level of performance, not by random chance, but by focused choice, over and over again.

It's not that difficult. Look at what my unbeliever was able to do within a few minutes of beginning to apply mental training techniques.

Remember: Powerful mental techniques are user-friendly and capable of delivering results very quickly.

Chapter 2: On Attitude

During one lesson, I noticed Leo-tai looking at me as if he was trying to decide whether I was really listening.

"A bad attitude can cost you everything, Danielsan; it affects not only how you feel, but also how you perform. This you must remember, for when you teach," he told me.

That's how he'd start sometimes. He would just throw something out to see if he'd caught my attention.

I remember teasing him once, saying, "I know when you do that."

"What?" he asked innocently.

"You know, check to see if I'm really listening."

"Really? And did you know that I know when you know that you think you know what I'm doing?"

The truth is: I was listening, it's just that his teaching method was so spontaneous that, no matter what mood I was coming from, I had to set it aside right away as he started, or I might accidentally offend the creative old soul . . . So, I responded, "What do you mean for when I teach?"

"Oh someday, I'm sure you will," he said. "Now, always remember, a Warrior/Champion learns how to control his internal mental climate. And having a good attitude helps him to achieve that control by creating an expectation of success. The right attitude helps empower him to take the necessary actions and to focus on the things that must be done—a good attitude can make all the difference."

"Why?" I asked. "What makes it so powerful?"

"The reason is quite simple," he said. "It's because a good attitude, a positive attitude, creates optimism, positive energy. And positive energy is much better at setting good things into motion than negative energy is. Warriors with negative attitudes become victims of their own negative outlook; they lose because their own negativity drains them. Winning has a lot to do with having a good attitude. Not only in competition, Danielsan, but also in life generally. You must always remember that."

Many years later my mind flashed back to that lesson.

I was dealing with an elite athlete trying to come to terms with a very tough competitive loss. While still deeply hurt, he asked me, "What's the use of working on keeping a positive attitude? It didn't seem to help me—did it?"

It's at times like these that I wish Leo-tai could step in. When an athlete is devastated one must tread lightly. I set out to try and explain what Leo-tai had taught me (and had somehow known that I would need to help someone else understand one day).

"Listen," I told him, "I know you're upset, and I also know how hard it is, because I've been on this path before you. But I'm here to tell you, as a wise old teacher once told me, that working on keeping a positive attitude is what will help you work through this bad patch. A positive attitude helps create the opportunity for a great comeback or for a great performance—A positive attitude never works against you. But a negative attitude will always find a way to work against you. Even if one finds a way to win despite a bad attitude, the fact is that he could always have performed better still."

Like Leo-tai used to do with me, I caught myself looking to see if my athlete was listening. I don't like to offer up what Leo-tai taught me if I sense someone is tuned out. In his case, he seemed to be listening, so I felt encouraged to go on.

"A champion teaches himself the skill of turning things around inside his head," I explained. "He learns how to look at a negative setback both as temporary, and even as an opportunity for positive change. He knows that the things he can learn from his loss will make him even better, even stronger, in the long run. The Mental Warrior learns from his setbacks and he doesn't allow them to distract him from reaching his true potential."

"So keep your self-talk positive. Keep your outlook positive. By doing so, you give yourself the best chance to perform well. Take on your inner feelings with courage and determination; never allow a bad attitude to hold you back from achieving the level of personal success that you are capable of."

"Never beat yourself up after a loss—there's always something positive to be gained, something to be learned, even from a negative situation."

I remember how after an especially tough and disappointing loss one of my kid champions summed it up. "I was doing well," he told me. "I'm better than he is. I'm not sure what happened—but next time he won't be so lucky."

"So you see? You must choose to stay positive," I told him. "Even a kid can do it."

"I know," he said slowly, "but right now, I just feel so bad, I feel so low."

I understood the heaviness in his heart, the disappointment, and as Leo-tai had taught me, I wanted him to understand that he had the power to turn this thing around in his head.

"Look, try this," I pointed up to the clock on the wall. "Give yourself just five more minutes to feel bad about this thing if you really feel you need to, and then after those five minutes are up, *decide* to start seeing the experience as an opportunity to help you figure out how to create a positive change in the level of your play. Turn it around in your head," I urged.

He looked up at me and nodded. Mental control starts with a *decision*. It was clear that we had a deal.

About five minutes later, I watched him walk out of that locker room right on time, just as I'd expected him to. You could tell by the way he walked that the decision had been made. The temporary setback had now become an opportunity for positive change. He had turned things around in his head. He was focused on the opportunities that lay ahead for positive change. He had *decided* that his attitude would be positive.

It's not always easy; it takes a decision, and a commitment to a different point of view.

Champions can do that—and so can you.

Remember: The Warrior/Champion understands that a bad attitude can cost him everything. It affects not only how you feel, but also how you perform.

Chapter 3: Gaining the Mental Edge

Sports psychology studies what successful people do. One of the most profound things, validated through study after study of many great athletes, is that if you take a group of athletes with equal ability and some receive mental training while others do not, the ones who were given mental training will always outperform those without. Why? Simple: because those who use mental training skills develop a Mental Edge.

Once, when I was young, my grandfather took me to see the legendary soccer player from Brazil—Pelé—at Tampa Stadium.

I'll never forget that warm summer night, as he dominated the game with three electrifying goals. That was a long time ago, but I'll always remember the way he dodged down the field, feinted and swerved on a dime to get past defenders, the ball seemingly glued to his feet—until he let it fly inside the goal posts.

Years later, I came across a story about Pelé in the writings of the late Gary Mack, a noted sports mental trainer with whom Pelé had shared what he considered to be the two keys to winning—Enthusiasm and a Mental Edge.

Pelé told Gary about the routine he used before every game he played. He would go into the locker room about an hour early and find a private corner in the locker room. Then he would lie down using a towel as a pillow and cover his eyes.

Pelé explained how he began to watch a film in his mind's eye: a film of himself as a kid playing soccer on the beach in Brazil. He let this "movie" bring back glorious memories of the sand, the warm sun on his back, the ocean breeze feathering his temples. He would vividly recall the thrill of the game, the joy that it brought to him; he would immerse himself in his love of the game, allowing himself to relive those glowing memories. Allowing himself to feel them.

In short, before every single game he played, Pelé made sure to put himself in touch with his pure love of his sport.

Then Pelé moved forward in his mental movie. Pelé described how he began to review and watch himself relive some of his greatest moments in world competitions. He talked about letting himself *feel* and enjoy the intensity of those winning feelings over and over again. He talked about how crucial it was for him to make a strong connection with those feelings and images in his past before he proceeded to imagine himself performing at his absolute peak in the upcoming event.

Finally, Pelé told Gary that he would see himself as he was about to become: playing brilliantly, scoring goals, dribbling past defenders in a mental movie made up of positive images with strong feelings of enjoyment and triumph. He imagined everything before it ever happened: the crowd, the atmosphere, the field, his own team, his opponents, he saw himself playing irresistibly like a champion—as a force that could not be stopped. But most important, he told Gary, was to remember that it was not just about vision and imagery, but also about *feeling* the emotions associated with success. He pointed out that he vividly imagined how good it all felt.

Only after about a half-hour of relaxation and mental rehearsal, would Pelé begin to stretch and prepare his muscles for the job they had to do. By then, he could relax because he had already primed his mind for victory. By the time he'd jogged into the stadium, he was (almost literally) unstoppable. Physically and mentally he was armed and fortified to win. No one could touch him.

In that short time with Gary, Pelé shared with us exactly how to tap into what he considered the two essential keys to winning: Enthusiasm and a Mental Edge.

I share this lesson with all my clients and suggest that they too create an internal place, a place where their minds can go before any event in order to rehearse, visualize, feel, and prepare exactly as Pelé used to. This is where you go to play and watch your mental highlight tapes; this is where you once again connect with the fun and love of your sport, to *feel* that winning feeling. Most of all, this is where you go to mentally prepare yourself and to gain the mental edge before battle.

For the athlete who's just starting out and who may not have past successes to replay, I suggest that they pretend that they do and that they watch themselves as if they did. After all, it's your movie! You're the director and producer, the editor and writer, and the more imagination you can squeeze into your movie the better. Mix in some enthusiasm with your imagery and now both of Pelé's keys to winning are in the formula. It's also important to practice seeing yourself overcoming adversity and staying in control whatever might arise. This doesn't make for arrogance—though it might sound like it. It creates confidence. Confidence is different from arrogance, and confidence is one of the keys to performing well.

Use the same routine that Pelé did to get things going for yourself. Practice mixing relaxation, imagery, feelings, and enthusiasm, prior to competition in a pre-game routine, in order to gain a mental edge and a sure sense of confidence going into the event. In this lesson, you have one of the most successful athletes in the world telling you how he went about preparing for competition.

Pearls of wisdom.

Remember: One must consistently practice mental skills and pre-game routines in order to tap one's full potential.

Chapter 4: Learning to Fly Navy Jets

Shortly after arriving at Aviation Officer's Candidate School in Pensacola, Florida, the young college grads get to meet their Drill Instructors.

The Marine Drill Instructors we had during those initial five months of aviation military indoctrination were the best the Marine Corps had to offer. These Drill Instructors had earned the right to be brought onboard Naval Aviation Schools Command, and their job was to seek out and eliminate any mentally weak candidates who may have found themselves wrongly assigned to the aviation program. They were methodical, effective, and professional in their approach, and they eventually got around to working on every single candidate. If you didn't have a mental game, you weren't likely to make it through. For those of us who survived, it was off to flight school as newly commissioned Naval Officers.

It wasn't long before one of my classmates sought me out for some advice regarding a certain flight instructor. Some of these instructors were pretty intense and the environment they created from the back seat of the cockpit could make the mental part of any training mission very challenging. At any rate, my friend John had been told that he had to do a flight over again. Not good. In fact, if that happened twice, he was in danger of being kicked out of flight school. In addition to that worry, he had some bad vibes about having to fly with that instructor again.

"Tell me what went wrong the last time," I suggested. "What was going through your head when it turned ugly?"

He tried to remember.

"Well, because of bad weather, I was being vectored all around, which shifted the entire training mission on the spot. As I sought to regain control of the situation I kept thinking: Why me, why do I get the lousy weather? What is this instructor's problem? Why is he gunning for me? What else can go wrong? What have I done to deserve all this hassle?"

John looked at me and shrugged. "You know how it is, some idiot instructor screaming at the top of his lungs, creating havoc, hitting switches, calling for emergency procedures, all that stuff!" John reflected for a second. "More than anything else, I remember feeling rushed."

"Since you felt rushed, you probably did rush," I told him, "and when that happens it interferes with our performance or whatever it is we're trying to do. Rushing automatically increases tension, which causes more mistakes to happen. More mistakes bring on more tension. It's a vicious cycle: the more mistakes we make, the more frustrating it becomes, and the easier it is for us to lose our mental focus . . . The rule is: don't rush when the pressure's on—smooth is fast. Breathe, pause, and learn to gather yourself—but never, ever, allow yourself to rush your game."

"I also remember that I began to second-guess myself," said John. "That didn't help either."

"Right. If you begin to over-analyze the situation, that can kick-start a lot of negative self-talk. I remember when my martial arts instructor Leo-tai would notice me doing this, he'd shake his head, and tell me that I needed to start by shutting down the negative self-talk, that I needed to quit fighting myself."

"How?" asked John.

"He taught me to interrupt any negative self-talk the instant I noticed it and replace it by firing off positive self-talk. Things like: *I'm fast, I'm focused, I'm good.* He always said not to let negative thoughts get in your way. You have to cancel the negativity and feed your self-belief instead. This will improve your concentration, and lower your level of tension, which will help you to perform better. Shutting down negative self-talk begins by interrupting it, and then instantly replacing it."

John was listening.

"That makes sense," he admitted. "Trouble is, I still think that this guy is out to get me personally."

"OK, so that makes him a serious opponent, and with a serious opponent you have to get a clear idea in your head of what you need in order to beat him. Once you are clear on what you must do to win, you have to stay focused on the most important task at hand, so that no matter what he throws at you—he's unable to disrupt your task-consciousness.

You can't let him rattle you, to come between you and what you intend to do. If he disrupts your task-consciousness, he wins—and you lose, especially in jet training. You've got to stay task-focused. You can't let your opponent take that from you."

"That's exactly what happened last time we went up," John admitted, "and that's what really worries me. You know how crazy it gets up there. We're moving really fast. Once he rattled me, it all went downhill. Frankly, I'm a little spooked having to fly with this instructor again. I imagine it feels kind of like having to fight some guy who knocked you down before."

"Anyone can land a lucky punch," I told him. "Snap out of it. The past does not equal the future! Leave your bad experience with this guy in the past, where it belongs. Don't sabotage your next performance by feeding your brain negative feelings about an event that is still out in the future.

The Art of Mental Training teaches that our performance action will follow the mental thoughts and images we entertain. In other words: you'll get what you see in your mind's eye. The brain helps you achieve your goals when you show it the results that you want it to produce for you, so be sure never to dwell on images or feelings of outcomes that you definitely don't want."

"Meaning?" asked John.

"Meaning that one of the most important things about competing at anything is learning how to enter a competition mentally prepared to do your best . . . Beyond shutting down the negative self-talk the instant it appears, I want you to work on connecting feelings and images of success with the precise event that lies before you. You have to show your mind what you want to have happen the next time you're flying with this instructor. And you have to start doing this type of mental training as far ahead of the actual event as possible."

Over the next couple of weeks, John set some time aside to practice some "Imagineering" (as you'll learn in a lesson that lies ahead) during daily relaxation sessions. During these times, he allowed only images and feelings of victory and success to be associated in his mind with the upcoming event when he would meet his opponent.

Using his mind's eye, he imagined himself, in great detail, as the ultimate military aviation professional doing his very best under situations of extreme pressure. He practiced seeing and feeling himself having an intense ability to stay task-conscious and task-focused—no matter what. He could even see and feel himself shutting down any negative self-talk the instant it arose and replacing it with empowering self-talk.

His efforts paid off! John later told me how he had beaten his opponent the next two times they had met over the next several weeks. Today, John is a seasoned captain flying with a major airline.

What this true story teaches us is that by using sports mental training techniques, you can overcome obstacles that might otherwise have stopped you from achieving goals that are important to you outside the realm of sports. In other words, when used correctly, mental techniques can help you achieve your dreams.

Remember: Stay task-focused. Interrupt negative self-talk and images the moment they arise, shut them down on the spot. Replace them with positive self-talk and positive images. Concentrate on showing your brain exactly what it is that you want to achieve, never dwell on what you do not want to happen.

Chapter 5: The Importance of Self-Belief

I remember once up in Washington State, Leo-tai and I were hiking along part of the Pacific Crest Trail. Leo-tai loved the beauty of those mountains. There we met a strange guy, possibly a young hermit, who bent our ears with wild-eyed warnings of aliens and UFO's all around the local wilderness after dark.

That night at camp, after joking and laughing about the guy's spooky alien stories, Leo-tai and I sensed the presence of . . . someone. We both stood up at the same moment and looked out into the dark. All around us at the edge of the darkness were many pairs of unblinking, yellowish eyes. I couldn't figure out what sort of creatures those eyes belonged to, but they were all around us in the dark, reflected by the light of our dying fire. I'm not going to lie: I felt a little nervous as I counted seven separate pairs of eyes.

Leo-tai was very calm, but I immediately started hurling rocks—hard. I figured if they were aliens, I was going to knock at least one of them out by cracking his skull with my rock-solid fastball.

Meanwhile, Leo-tai fanned the fire back to life.

"You better help me out here," I urged him. "They're not going away!"

Leo-tai turned from the fire and started throwing rocks with focused accuracy. Not bad for an old guy, I thought. Still, we were so outnumbered it was scary, and the silence of the creatures all around us was very unnerving. Then, suddenly, we caught a glimpse of whom we were facing.

A pack of huge, fearless, marauding raccoons! They were wild, they were mean, and they were coming in—clearly wanting some food. We fought hard as they repeatedly charged us and tried to intimidate us into running. They seem to have absolutely no fear of us at all. I wondered if they had rabies.

After several minutes of charges and counter-attacks, Leo-tai somehow sensed who the leader of the pack was. And paying no attention to several closer raccoons, he caught him right between the eyes with a rock travelling at the speed of sound. It was the most accurate shot anyone could have asked for.

Bang! "Who wants some!?" Leo-tai exclaimed. The leader rocked back, stunned, and then quickly took off running, with his entire pack behind him.

"Great shot," I said, breathing hard. "But what was that all about? Since when do raccoons run around behaving like that?"

Leo-tai smiled shaking his head. "A very fearless group they were."

Then he asked me a question, "Danielsan, did you ever think that we weren't going to win?"

I thought back.

"Not really," I said. "All I knew was that this was darn serious, that it was time to fight, and that fighting was exactly what I was going to do."

My teacher smiled.

"Very good, Danielsan. Self-belief. You must always begin by believing that you have what it takes. When the pressure is on, the more you believe in yourself, the better your performance will be. Without strong self-belief, the warrior winds up nowhere. You have to believe that you can win, then that self-belief puts you in a position to win."

"Are you're talking about confidence?" I asked.

"Not completely. Confidence is a by-product of strong self-belief. The more powerful his self-belief, the more confidence the warrior is able to summons up when the pressure is on. And the stronger his self-belief, the better his performance will be."

"So self-belief brings on a confidence that can empower us?"

"Indeed. When you really believe that you can win, Danielsan, something extremely powerful is set into motion.

So, in order to help build the strongest self-belief system he can have, a Warrior/Champion learns to use imagination to see himself in his mind's eye accomplishing his most desired success while in a deep relaxed state of awareness. This is the key to improving self-belief, the foundation of which lies deep inside the mind."

What Leo-tai meant was that while our self-belief system is formed over the years by experiences, memories, and outside influences—anyone can still refine and build up his own self-belief system by using the tools of relaxation and imagination. The champion sees and feels himself succeeding in his mind's eye, many times over, long before he actually arrives for the competition. This is how he improves his self-belief from inside.

"Teach them, Danielsan, that the Warrior/Champion goes within."

And with that Leo-tai disappeared behind the flaps of his tent.

Hmmm, I thought. That's kind of dramatic. What's he thinking? He must be very sure that I have no questions to ask—and that the pack of raccoons aren't coming back.

"Hey, does that mean you're done for the night?" I asked him.

"Hasta mañana," said the voice from inside the tent. "I am much older than you my friend—and I'm tired."

I couldn't help but asking him just one more question.

"Okay," I said, "but what if the raccoons come back again?"

Without hesitation, came the reply, "Why—the answer is quite clear, Danielsan. If they attack again . . . then they shall lose again."

Remember: It's self-belief that gets everything going.

Chapter 6: Imagineering & Self-Confidence

Imagineering—the technique of showing our minds how we want things to go, and a term first made famous by the legendary dreamer, Walt Disney. We should all take his advice and allow ourselves to practice sensory rich Imagineering. Champions use Imagineering prior to their events. It's also often used by people in order to help them achieve the successful completion of a project or an important goal over time. This simple practice has been proven to be so essential and so effective that the athlete who fails to practice the technique apparently never plays to his true potential. (Interestingly, the same results have been observed with actors and musicians as well.) For performance of any kind, mental preparation is as important as physical training. So, if you leave "Imagineering" out of your preparation, you will be hurting yourself and helping your opponent.

Imagine stepping into competition having seen and felt the entire experience before, from the crowd to the coaches, from the venue to your own performance, all in your own mind. It's a fascinating experience. It creates an incredible feeling of confidence.

What's really the key with Imagineering is that you not only see and watch, but that you actually *feel* yourself succeeding, over and over again. Make sure that you bring emotion into your mental practice. Practice feelings along with images including those related to your overcoming adversity and being able to successfully fight your way out of challenging predicaments or situations.

Never allow yourself to entertain images or feelings of defeat during your Imagineering sessions. This is because whatever impressions reach the subconscious mind it will accept as being true—and what it believes to be true affects your performance. Feed it empowering, successful images and feelings, and it delivers performance, drive, and motivation from deep within yourself in line with those images and feelings.

However, if you feed it suggestions of worries or failure then you will defeat yourself—with no other opponent necessary.

Success, victory, and your ability to effectively overcome adversity is what you must rehearse, rehearse, and rehearse again. Relax, be still, and in your mind—you must see it, *feel* it, and accept that it is coming your way. This process of conditioning for success sets things in motion. It creates confidence and confidence is one of the most significant by-products of good mental training. The most powerful confidence comes as the result of both physical *and* mental preparation, and winning and achievement has everything to do with preparation.

If you think you're confident now, and you're not using mental training techniques, then you really can't even begin to know what you're missing or understand how much you stand to improve with mental training—that insight comes only through its practice.

Remember: Imagineering is vital because it leads to greater self-belief and greater confidence, which in turn leads to better performance and achievements.

Chapter 7: The Critical Three

Breathing, relaxation, and imagery are mentioned throughout the lessons so often because they're such fundamentally important tools for the Warrior/Champion. I call them "The Critical Three." I remember how often Leo-tai spoke of all three. They're all crucial in order to help create the Ideal Mental Climate from which peak performance springs forth.

Sometimes clients tend to get over-analytical about the "right" way to practice breathing or the "right" way to go deep into relaxation. It's always fun to show them that in reality, it's much easier than they ever thought it could be.

First, let's learn about breathing.

I have a memory of Leo-tai from a time when I had been watching him high up on a mountain, and so near the edge that I worried he might fall. He was practicing what he called his focused breathing, his hands sometimes flowing to the rhythm of his breathing in slow and balanced circular motions, and sometimes not.

He had taught me to do just as he was doing, to draw the air in deeply and slowly to the bottom of my lungs through my nose, while expanding the diaphragm. Then, after holding it momentarily, he slowly pushed the air out of the lungs by drawing the diaphragm in. He explained that it's important to let the air out through a relaxed and slightly opened mouth while keeping the tip of the tongue pressed lightly against the ridge behind the front teeth, with the tongue touching the roof of the mouth.

Afterwards, I asked him what was going through his mind as he practiced his breathing.

"Nothing," he said, "I just observe my breathing. That's all. If a thought comes to me, I pay it no attention and it soon flows away. The more I focus on the breathing, the more I observe the breathing, the quieter my thoughts become. And also, notice that I can practice the breathing without any form whatsoever, whenever I need."

"What do you mean, without any form?" I asked.

"I can practice my focused breathing whenever I want, even now as I sit and visit with you," he told me. "I practice focused breathing to help keep me centered—to help bring me back to the present. I can do it without form. You do not see me moving around or flowing as a tai-chi master does do you? Yet still I am practicing my focused breathing."

I'll never know why, but the sureness and simplicity of the words that he spoke that day have never left me. I'm grateful for that because I've learned through experience that it's through the focused breathing that he taught me that I've always been able to begin to achieve the mental control or focus that was required for whatever serious challenge I may have been facing at the time.

So, from now on, whenever focused breathing is mentioned in any of our other lessons, you'll know exactly what we are describing, how it's done, and why it's part of the mix of tools that helps us achieve mental control. It's important to practice focused breathing if one hopes to ever be able to harness the power of the technique.

There is a second important concept mentioned throughout *The Art of Mental Training* that Leo-tai never tired of explaining, time and time again, year after year. Let me explain as he did to me: the concept of relaxation . . . both mental and physical.

What do we mean by relaxation? And why is relaxation practice so important for the athlete and Mental Warrior? Relaxation matters because when used with mental imagery it facilitates and allows our inner (subconscious) mind to clearly see our success imagery and feel our success feelings.

It's only when we are in a deep state of relaxation that the conscious mind quits acting as a filter for the inner mind. It's when the critical conscious mind is set aside through relaxation (for several minutes) that our Imagineering can reach the inner mind directly. Among other things, the inner mind is a goal-striving mechanism. Show it your goals through imagery and with feelings of them as having already been accomplished . . . and it sets out to help you make it so. It accepts the input as being true. Seemingly saying to itself, if this is true, then these must be the actions that I must be taking that help make it so.

And that's critically important because by blending breathing, relaxation and the third critical element, Imagineering, the mental athlete is able to tap an inner resource designed to help him achieve his goals.

Coming from within, your motivation and volition become stronger and more focused. From within, you'll soon find yourself more easily doing all the things that need to be done in order for you to accomplish your goals. When the inner mind is able to see what you want, it's able to help you get what you want. Relaxation skills are what open up the lines of communication between the inner mind and your Imagineering. Proper breathing helps you go deeper into relaxation whenever you so desire.

So, what does relaxation practice entail? And how do you practice setting up these lines of communication?

The ability to achieve a state of deep relaxation easily and quickly comes only through practice. After a few weeks of practice, one can usually enter a deep state of relaxation within a few minutes of deciding to do so—and for some it can happen even quicker than that.

I tell my clients to consider practicing and developing this skill by using the following process. I remind them that if they just allow the process to happen naturally, then it will. You can't try to force relaxation, but with practice anyone can learn how to slip into relaxation quite easily.

Move to a quiet space where you won't be disturbed. Lie down on your back with your feet slightly apart, arms slightly extended from your body, palms facing down, and make sure you are as comfortable as possible before proceeding. (In other words: no tight or restrictive clothing, temperature not too hot, not too cold, etc. Get comfortable).

Now, fix your eyes on a point above you on the ceiling. Remaining as still as you can, begin by taking three long, deep, deep, breaths, inhaling through your nose. Hold each breath temporarily, and then exhale slowly through your mouth. And with each breath that you release, I want you to feel a wave of relaxation begin to overwhelm you as you let go and begin to enjoy the process.

As you exhale the third breath, gently let your eyelids begin to close. Now, for the next ten breaths, imagine your eyelids getting heavier and heavier. I want you to mentally repeat the word "deeper" as you exhale and let all tension and thoughts disappear every time you breathe out. Let yourself go deeper into relaxation with each breath that you let out.

If your mind drifts, that's okay; just gently bring your attention back to learning how to relax and how to let go as you exhale and mentally repeat the word "deeper" slowly to yourself. After ten easy breaths, you are ready to begin focusing on relaxing the muscles of every part of your body.

Start with your toes and begin moving up your body as total relaxation begins to take over. Focus on relaxing each and every muscle in your body. From toes to calves, to thighs, to abs, to chest, to back, to arms, to shoulders, and even to your neck: every muscle letting go and completely relaxing. Continue all the way up to the scalp and facial muscles. Visualize each muscle loosening, and feel a wave of deep relaxation flowing deeply into all of your muscles, into all of your body. Allow yourself to go deeper into relaxation with each breath that you take.

Don't rush it, don't force it; simply allow your muscles to turn loose, go limp and relax naturally as you experience the serenity of total relaxation. (Sometimes clients tell me that a leg or arm twitched or moved involuntarily for an instant and they ask me about it. That's nothing to be concerned about; it's only the deep hidden tension being triggered and released from where it has been hiding. The release of this hidden tension is both therapeutic and healthy.)

Now, allow yourself to enjoy this state of relaxation for about twenty minutes, maybe a little more. Drift in this sea of healthy relaxation and during this time, while in this deeply relaxed state, watch yourself as in a movie, and project images in your mind's eye of you achieving what you desire. See it as being true. Feel it. Show your mind through images and feelings what you will accomplish. See it clearly. Watch yourself accomplishing it. Experience it inwardly as if it were already true.

Remember that now, through deep relaxation, you've opened a direct channel to your subconscious mind. Feed it images and feelings of success in your "movies" that it will then set out to help you accomplish. With this practice, you are setting a powerful force in motion from deep inside that will help propel you towards the success you envision.

After twenty minutes or so of deep relaxation and "success conditioning" through your use of your mental images and feelings, it's time to either bring yourself back to a state of full awareness—or else time to simply allow yourself to slip into restful sleep. That's up to you.

If it's time to sleep, just let yourself doze off. However, if you need to bring yourself back to a state of full awareness, then this is an easy way to do it. Imagine a staircase with five steps going up. See yourself slowly climbing up the steps, and tell yourself that with each step you take that you feel more refreshed, more alert, and more aware. And, that when you reach the top step, you'll feel relaxed, refreshed, and rejuvenated, completely alert, and ready to carry on with your day.

When you reach the last step, let your eyelids open, inhale

completely, and stretch. (Of course, if you are practicing your relaxation during the day within a busy schedule— there's no harm in using an alarm clock just to help ensure that you get back to your schedule on time in case the deep relaxation ever leads to an unscheduled nap.)

That's how the Mental Warrior uses breathing, relaxation and success imagery. He doesn't use them only once. Instead, he incorporates them into his training routine using repetition over several weeks and months, so that the success conditioning has a chance to actually be absorbed by the subconscious mind and to take root, thus helping to improve self-belief, self-confidence and performance. Through practice like this, the Mental Warrior is able to engage and use the power of his subconscious mind in order to help him achieve his goals.

Remember what Leo-tai once told me: "The Mental Warrior learns about focused breathing, relaxation, and imagery—and then he sets off to actually use them."

Chapter 8: The Mental Warrior

I saw a flash of silver as he drew his gun from behind the small of his back. My gun already drawn, I was behind cover. He was stuck out in the open; I had a clear line of fire. He looked about forty years old, with dark, deep-sunken eyes—he looked every bit the criminal he was. I had tracked and chased him down. With my team not far behind me, he was now cornered. The adrenaline surged inside my body. Twenty-five feet away was a fugitive felon with a gun in his hand thinking about using it on me.

"Drop it," I told him firmly, without for one instant ceasing to bear my gaze straight down my pistol sight.

Out drawn, and out positioned, there wasn't that much for him to think about. Either he wanted to live or he wanted to die, that's really all he had to decide. He knew it was over. He lowered his weapon. Once we had him in cuffs and sped off to our location, it hit me. At last, the murderous drug lord who had cost the life of one of our agents was finally in custody.

To this day, I credit Leo-tai's training as the one thing that most helped me keep the hair-trigger on my government-issued 9mm from engaging, and sending five or six black talon law enforcement rounds straight into their target—center mass.

What a crazy job this is, I remember thinking, as I sat down for a moment to let the energy subside. And as I did, my mind flashed back to a time when Leo-tai once described the Mental Warrior to me . . .

We were walking in the hills, he leading as usual, with that untiring pace that sometimes even I had trouble keeping up with. It was hot, and I enjoyed the breeze as we climbed higher and the humidity began to drop.

When we finally reached the top of the trail, we stopped, rested, and admired the view as he told me what he had planned to tell me.

"Danielsan," he said, "in order to become a Mental Warrior, you must learn to recognize the Mental Warrior; you must understand where the training takes you."

He had my undivided attention.

This is what he told me: "Mental Warriors cannot be intimidated. Their self-confidence is too deeply rooted to be shakeable. They arrive on the scene to dominate. They love to compete; competing energizes them. They repel negative thoughts; they control their internal environment. They know how to remain focused under even the most challenging conditions."

He told me: "Mental Warriors make it a point to be ready. They've learned to manage pressure; they never fail to keep moving forward. They refuse to lose, they'll never quit, and they will patiently work to find a solution and to find a way to win. Mental Warriors cannot accept not trying."

Leo-tai went on: "Mental Warriors are goal oriented. They know what they want to do and set out to achieve it. Their dreams and goals motivate them to excel. They are dedicated. They know how to control their emotions so as to not allow them to sabotage their own performance. Mental Warriors never lose their composure and self-control in the heat of battle."

"Most of all, Mental Warriors are brave, Danielsan, they have heart. They have the courage and inner strength to achieve their full potential. They understand the power of imagination, concentration, and consistency."

He closed his lesson that day by reminding me that the only way that one could ever become a Mental Warrior was by practicing what the Art teaches.

Remember: One must practice in order to become.

Chapter 9: Controlling Anger

"Let's review, Danielsan," he told me as we sat down. Sometimes after a workout, we'd drink some tea and enjoy the view from his simple patio overlooking the coastline.

"At this point, you understand that—whether positive, negative, or anywhere in between—all emotions are created by what we are thinking. You understand that the stronger the warrior is able to build his self-belief system, the better. You understand that self-belief, a good attitude, confidence, and positive self-talk are what "get things going." You understand that emotions affect performance. So, if bad emotions arise, you understand there are ways you can learn to control their impact on your performance. Right?"

"Roger that."

He gave me an odd look.

"Yes," I corrected.

"Good. Then you also know how imagery, focused

breathing, and relaxation all help to give us a mental edge over the competition."

"Very tricky," I teased him.

"Be serious now, Danielsan, and pay close attention, because today we must talk about anger . . . We all get angry; this is normal. Yet you must always remember that if the warrior does not control his anger it will always end up controlling him. And when that happens, victory will be much more difficult. You see, anger is an emotional response. Before the emotion is allowed to take control, the warrior must redirect its energy. Real champions work to develop an ability to control their anger so that it cannot hurt their performance."

I grappled with this: "Do you mean that they end up no longer feeling this kind of emotion?"

"Not at all. I mean that they have learned how to channel such an emotion so that it won't affect their focus and performance in a negative way. With anger, once the emotion comes up—or boils up!—real champions make a deliberate choice to use the energy, but they do not allow themselves to lose control to it or fall victim to it."

"How?"

"They ask themselves, 'Who is in charge here?—Me? Or this fury inside myself?' By that simple act, the warrior spirit begins to regain control. And that control begins with a simple choice, a decision. The warrior *decides* to channel the anger into making his resolve stronger still. He redirects the anger into tough play. He creates a stronger resolve to beat the competition and to raise his own level of play. Rather than losing control to the anger, he becomes like a smiling assassin; he's mad, yes, but it's a cool, calculating mad. He is using the intensity and the passion of the emotion, yet he doesn't lose control to it. The champion knows that in order to perform well, he must stay in control. How else can he expect to control his performance?"

"OK, so how does one manage the intensity of the emotion?" I asked him.

"It always starts with a choice to not let it control you," said Leo-tai. "Concentrate and use focused breathing to help manage the intensity. Use internal self-talk with suggestions like: *Stay Cool, Relax, Be Calm* — to help you stay in control. Imagery and relaxation techniques are also powerful tools that can be used to manage the intensity of an anger reaction. All of these—worked on and practiced—will help. But there must first, always be a choice."

"And Danielsan, if you should ever feel that you must vent your anger, remember that it's better to do it privately, so that you do not shake the confidence of the team's trust in you. To let them see you lose control, even if you felt you needed it for yourself, can only hurt that trust."

Remember: If anger arises, make the decision to not let it control you. Use techniques to redirect the energy; use the energy to make your resolve stronger. Become like the smiling assassin that sees his mark.

Chapter 10: Shots Fired

All the typical, normal radio traffic was abruptly shattered. "Shots fired! Shots fired! Agent down! One Zero Eight to Control we need help! Agent down!"

On calls like that the com-center responds with a three beep burst that signals everyone to clear the airwaves. Three loud "Beeeeeps", and then: "All units standby—shots fired, shots fired. One Zero Eight say your location."

"One Zero Eight near the northwest corner of 5th and Hines—Location 3, we've been ambushed! Agent down with a head wound! Agent down!" You could hear gunfire over the radio, while the emotion in his voice sent chills down my spine.

"Repeat—we are pinned down, we need backup, we need paramedics at Location 3. Two Zero Nine is down with a head wound. Oh my God—hurry—send help!"

"All units, all units, shots fired, agent down, location 3, all units respond," directed the voice from the com-center.

The call struck me like a punch in the face. I shook off my disbelief and jumped into action. I was partnering with the case agent that night—an experienced and highly respected veteran. Jake and I looked at each other. Those were our guys on the radio. This was really happening to us. A routine surveillance had turned deadly without warning.

Within minutes other agencies of our Federal task force and the local police were responding. They began to as quickly as possible set up a perimeter barrier around the area in order to keep the shooter contained. Paramedics and all available units were on the way.

The idea is to close the perimeter. No one gets in or out. One of the task force agencies began to set up a command post at nearby parking lot.

High-level narcotics traffickers can be ruthlessly violent. Tonight they'd proved it once again. My heart was pounding as we raced towards the scene.

When something like this happens, the only people on the radio should be those that are on the scene. Everyone else should be listening for details. Where are the shots coming from? Which direction should we not approach from? Where is the downed agent? The goal is to clear a path to him, push back any attack, and render immediate aid.

By the time we sped on to the scene, it was getting dark, the perimeter was in place, and there was an airship overhead. Our immediate goal was to reach the agent who had been shot. As we approached there was a patrol car guarding the part of the perimeter that blocked our access.

"Can't go in," said one of the officers.

We identified ourselves with credentials and badges.

Despite that he still refused: "Sorry, guys. The command post says no one in or out."

"The command post? Listen, I'm the case agent," Jake asserted. "I'm telling you to move your vehicle or I'll push it out of the way with my car. Do you understand? We have an agent down in there and his partner is calling for help. We're going in!"

The officer complied, moving his car. As he closed the perimeter behind us once again, the airship above immediately noticed us entering and came on the radio asking us to ID ourselves. (Our undercover cars didn't have large identifying numbers on the roof as police cars do.)

"Fed 2-7 is rolling in," I responded.

"Air -3 to Shop 2-7, be advised that you're heading into the kill-zone. Stop. Do not proceed. Back up."

Jake grabbed the mic from my hand. "Air-3,—Fed 2-7. Point us to where the agents are—repeat—direct us to the location of the downed agent."

"Roger 2-7, continue moving straight ahead—northbound," but before they could tell us how far ahead, or anything more, the command post stepped on the airship's transmission.

"Fed 2-7, you are to report to the command post immediately."

Jake and I looked at each other, wondering who was sending these orders to us.

"Fed 2-7 report back to the command post immediately— acknowledge!"

Jake was thinking. Finally, Jake responded.

"Negative CP, Fed 2-7 will not leave the area. We're going in to find our agents."

"2-7, exit the area immediately—we are waiting for a SWAT team. That's an order!" barked the voice over the radio.

"Negative," was Jake's instant response as he turned the volume down and looked over at me.

By this time, we'd both recognized the voice as that of a supervisory agent who just happened to be dating the Assistant US Attorney assigned to the task force. For some reason, he thought he was in charge. The reality was that he was from another agency, and his own training was flawed. His experience with things like this was zero, zip, nada, yet he'd dared to assume control. It was clear that the other agencies liked his idea of waiting around until a special tactical team could arrive. After all, no one could say for sure where the shooter was.

"Okay, he's keeping everybody out and they're listening to him. We aren't going to get any help from them. They're afraid. If we go back to the command post, we'll be taken out of the picture. Are you ready to move forward and do this with me?" Jake asked.

"Let's go," I told him. "The chopper said straight ahead."

Then suddenly—two more shots rang out. We both ducked instinctively. Our guys were still under fire.

With the sniper still out there, our best chance of reaching our guys safely and perhaps spotting the sniper's muzzle flash would be if we were on foot. We had our vests, our MP-5's, our 9mm's, radios and flashlights. We spilt up and started to move carefully up the street on different sides, using the darkness, the cars, the trees and the shrubs as cover. We moved in the direction that we'd been told our guys would be, using the tight orbits of the airship overhead as a general guide. Until finally, about another block away in the darkness, we saw what looked like one of our cars. We moved towards it. It was their car.

When we arrived at the scene, the horrible degree of injury I saw on my friend made me angry. The other agent, holding his partner's head together, looked up at us blankly and in shock. We had snuck up on him. He was dazed. "I thought you guys weren't coming, How come they aren't coming in?" he asked. "What took you so long? Where's the backup? Why aren't they coming in?" He was distraught as he continued holding his partners head together kneeling next to him, and just kept repeating, "I thought you guys weren't coming. I thought no one was coming."

"Look at me," Jake told him as we all crouched low along side of the vehicle. "We're here. There was never a point when we weren't coming. Now listen to me. Tell us where the shots came from." The agent pointed. While Jake rendered aid and tried to gather more information, I scanned the darkness and called in our exact location.

"Fed 2-7 to command post we need back-up and a rescue ambulance at location 3. We are two houses south from the corner, we are on the west side—expedite."

"Negative," replied the command post.

"Fed 2-7 needs a rescue ambulance now! Agent down with a head wound," I growled into the radio.

"Negative," was the reply. "You guys went in against orders, now you can bring him out on your own. No one else goes in until SWAT secures the area."

I glanced over at Jake, my blood was boiling.

This was unbelievable. Seasoned agents and police officers were listening to this and standing by acting like cowards while "Agent Down" calls were being ignored because an incompetent with rank had taken control of a trailer labeled "Command Post" and had *conveniently* put them all on the sidelines.

Jake's cell phone began to ring. By now, several more of our own guys had begun arriving on the edge of the perimeter, and having heard the radio transmissions, started calling Jake directly. They began to penetrate the perimeter just as we had and worked their way in towards us using their cars as targets while we watched for muzzle flash. After helping us move the injured agent and his shell-shocked partner into one of the vehicles that had worked its way to us, we transported our guys out of the kill zone without any help from the other agencies that were standing by.

On the way out, we had to start rescue breathing and CPR. By the time we arrived at the command post, we were drenched in blood. We hurriedly transferred the agent into the ambulance.

Not sending in the rescue ambulance like we'd requested had cost our colleague precious time. Jake was on his cell phone when we both saw him coming. "Stay cool," Jake advised me.

With no concern for our agent, the incompetent supervisory agent made his statement, "You're both relieved of duty," he told us, waving his arm like some sort of magician. "You're both off this case."

Jake ignored him as he put his cell phone away and jumped

inside the rescue ambulance that was beginning to roll away with the injured agent. He looked back at me.

"Secure the crime scene," he yelled. "I just activated the SWAT team and the dogs." And then he was gone.

"What?" I repeated, amazed. I just couldn't believe it. The dogs and the SWAT team hadn't even been called?

While calling around for help, Jake discovered that the command post had yet to even put out a call for a tactical unit. I felt a violent anger taking over.

When I turned expecting to confront the "incompetent in charge," he was already headed back to the command post trailer. Our guys looked at me. At that instant, I could see things going in a very bad direction. I didn't want to do what Leo-tai's teachings were telling me to do—but I did— and I let him go. I watched the supervisory agent and his side-kick step back inside the trailer.

It was time to re-focus. "Let's go secure the crime scene," I told our guys. And back we cautiously went into the kill zone once again, until the tactical team and the dogs eventually arrived and finally declared the area free of any snipers. The shooter was gone.

I'd just made it back to the command post area when Jake's call came through from the hospital. He let me know that our friend had died.

I remember how I looked at the command post trailer and

then forced myself to walk across the street to separate myself from it.

I remember sitting down and leaning up against a tree in somebody's front yard that night as my feelings of grief began to mix in with the anger that I felt towards the supervisor who had flatly refused to let the rescue ambulance in.

I remember thinking how these feelings seemed much too potent for any man with a gun to have going through his head.

I remember how I used focused breathing and Leo-tai's wisdom that night to help keep me from confronting that supervisory agent.

I remember thinking, and telling myself how this wasn't over . . .

But that for tonight—right now,—it had to be over.

Remember: You must choose to control anger through a decision. For if you lose control to anger—then the anger will surely control you.

Chapter 11: On Losing

(Following several months of investigation, the shooter from the previous story was later apprehended and convicted, the incompetent supervisory agent was forced out, and my partner Jake received another commendation.)

Mental athletes understand that they can't always control what takes place during an event. Things don't always go the way we'd like, no matter however well (and however hard) we've prepared. How we deal with that reality—and how we choose to look at the situation always affects what lies ahead for us.

So, even though we can't always control the way things unfold, at least we can always control the way we respond to the event. Mental warriors focus on what they can control, not on the "what ifs" or the "if only." Being able to choose how one responds to an unwelcome event is a critical skill. It has everything to do with how well we get on with our game—and even with our lives.

Mental athletes know that nobody wins all of the time. Not in life, not in sports. When things don't go their way, they know it's OK to be disappointed. What's not OK is dwelling on the disappointment.

Champions keep it in perspective. They are able to accept responsibility and recognize the situation as a temporary setback nothing more, nothing less. Yes it hurts, so they look at it, learn from it, and then let it go. I've lost myself, of course. In fact, that was how I met Leo-tai in the first place.

I was a young martial artist competing in tournaments and I'd just lost a major international competition—worse still, one that I'd been really expecting to win. I was having a tough time with the loss.

People kept telling me, "You still did great!" But runner-up wasn't what I'd wanted to be. As time went by, in response to my annoyance with myself, my training tailed off, my determination flagged, and everything seemed either too boring or too difficult to fuss about. I was slacking off.

I remember an older kid asking me once if I had ever heard of Coach Leo.

"I don't think so," I said. "What does he teach?"

"Mostly Shaolin—Chinese Kickboxing, but he teaches other things too. He really helped me once with my training."

"So, how'd he help then?" I asked, interested.

"Call him, here's his number. He only teaches small classes. Tell him you know me."

I carried that sheet of paper around with me for about two weeks. Finally I thought, "Well, what have I got to lose?" I called him and told him about myself. Coach Leo listened quietly on the phone, so much so that I began to wonder if he'd wandered off or hung up.

"Come tomorrow," he told me, and that ended our conversation.

When the next day came, I almost didn't go. I kept asking myself, "Why did I call this coach?" I was looking for a reason to miss our appointment. But before I knew it, and despite my best efforts to talk myself out of it, I wound up knocking on his door and then there he was. A medium-sized, elderly, rather stoic figure, his face calm and genuine.

"Danielsan," he said, and paused.

"Daniel what?"

"Daniel*san*. You look very much like your older brother, please come in," he said.

"You knew my brother?" I asked. Then suddenly I realized that I had indeed heard of Coach Leo before! Only I had never heard him called that because my brother had always called him Leo-tai. As far back as I can remember, Leo-tai had always taught my older brother how to fight. My brother was teaching me when he was drafted and sent to

73

Vietnam. After we lost him in the war, as I grew up I'd often found myself wondering about Leo-tai. And now, as fate would have it, so many years later, here he was in front of me, my brother's old instructor. Was this a coincidence? Head spinning, I stepped inside. I looked around. He appeared to live as simply as a monk.

Somehow I found it easy to be honest with him, knowing how my brother had loved him. After some tea, and having brought him up to date with the narrative of my tournament loss, I finished. He smiled and then spoke.

"This loss—you must let it go. True champions keep such a loss in perspective," he said. "You must look at it long enough to learn from it—but then you must let it go."

"Easier said than done," I thought, but what a powerful idea just the same. "Let it go." I let his advice sink in.

"Let it go," I told myself, and I slowly began to allow the weight of the loss to get lifted from my shoulders.

Learn from it—and let it go. What could be simpler, or more healing, than that?

But he wasn't finished with me yet. He leaned forward as if to make sure I was paying attention.

"Remember that champions never play the blame game. They pick themselves up and start working on what's coming up next. They hold their heads high, even when that isn't easy to do. They push themselves to move forward.

They know that this is how it has to be . . . They never forget that if you don't fail sometimes, then you probably aren't challenging yourself at a high enough level."

At the door, he said with a smile, "I want you to pick yourself up Danielsan; I want you to persist. Once you are ready to do so, then come back."

And that was the beginning of my friendship with Leo-tai.

I remember leaving his simple home that night and thinking of how glad I was at having found my brother's teacher so many years later. I was still only a teenager, and I knew that I was just at the beginning, but I'll never forget the feeling I had as I walked back the way that I had come. It was the feeling of knowing, somehow, that my life had just taken an unexpected and most interesting turn.

Remember: Champions focus on what they can control. They know that while they can't always control what takes place during an event, they can always control how they respond to an event. Within every setback lies the hidden opportunity for a great comeback.

Chapter 12: Fear of Failure

Ask yourself this: what type of competitor are you? Are you the kind who likes to play it safe and just do alright? Or are you the kind who's willing to take a chance on possibly failing in order to accomplish something amazing? More than anything else, it's a fear of failure that keeps people from achieving their full potential in sports, in life, in business—in everything.

Fearing failure is more than just a bad thing. The bottom line is that in order to be good in your sport, or whatever it is that you do, you simply can't be afraid of failing. Here's why: Being afraid to fail actually helps create the conditions that make failure more likely!

Fear of failure causes a lot of problems. It restricts you. The wrong types of thoughts result in shortness of breath, tight muscles, and an overload of stress . . . Worse still, fear of failing can cause a competitor to start playing it safe. Instead of rising up to meet the challenge, he subconsciously shrinks from it.

On the other hand—and this is the important point—once a competitor learns to overcome the fear of failing, his chances of succeeding increase dramatically.

In reality, fear of failure is nothing more than a perceived psychological threat to your ego and self-esteem. What typically causes a fear of failing is the state of mind that takes hold when a competitor is afraid of looking bad, or else is such a perfectionist that he's become overly self-critical. In either case, his internal state ends up holding him back, whether he's aware of it or not.

Adults are more than capable of wrecking their own chances with fear of failure. However, with a child, parents and coaches must be extra careful. Often the adults are the ones creating this build-up of nervous stress in the child athlete's internal world. Injecting the wrong emotional input into a child's occasional failure can ruin the child's love of the sport and even destroy their confidence.

With children, it's especially crucial that we help build self-esteem, not tear it down. Parents need to go easy on the criticism. Parents shouldn't act out. It's that type of adult behavior that can cause a child's fear of failure.

In order to avoid the internal state that causes the fear of failure, the mental athlete must first come to look at failure in an entirely different way from most people. He has to learn to accept that the only way to accomplish anything great is to risk failing at it first. He has to accept that without occasional failures he can never hope to get better. He has to understand that on the path to greatness, some failures are inevitable. And when he does lose, the mental athlete has to make a conscious decision to learn from that failure. Rather than abandoning himself to the luxury of misery, he will methodically shut down that destructive voice of internal self-criticism in favor of looking at failure as valuable feedback.

Thus, when he experiences failure he learns what, out of all his training, still isn't working. He learns how to fail constructively. In other words, the mental athlete won't allow a fear of failure to hold him back from greatness. By learning to look at the occasional failure differently, top competitors are able to enter competition without a fear of failure. And that is critically important. When there is no fear of failure, one gains an important advantage. An advantage that can make all the difference.

After all, consider this: there is no one in history, in or outside of sports, who ever rose to greatness without having once failed. Politicians have lost elections. Generals have lost battles. Millionaires have failed in prior business ventures. Behind every Olympic gold medal lie hundreds of second and third place finishes.

Think about it.

Remember: Fear of failure is caused by not knowing how to fail constructively. The only way to accomplish anything great is to risk failing at it first. If you have a fear of failing, it's more than just a bad thing. It can actually cripple your chances of success.

Chapter 13: Controlling Fear

One day he asked me about fear.

"Inside the eye of a cyclone, Danielsan, there is peace—while just outside, the cyclone unleashes all its fury and power. This is how it must be for the Mental Warrior also."

I told him how I'd once been so aware of fear that I sensed how it could become overwhelming. During my aviation training in the Navy, I admit that I got to know the type of fear that near-drowning can bring on. I nearly drowned on a couple of occasions during training. The truth is, try as they might to keep it from happening, people die in that type of training program every year. It's just the nature of the situation.

All the deep-water survival training is done wearing full flight gear including helmet and boots, with no floatation. You have to use the techniques taught and learn to avoid drowning despite everything that's weighing you down and trying to pull you under. It can be exhausting. One day, thanks to my lack of technique, I learned what the fear associated with believing you are going to drown felt like. I remember the dark green glaze of the water, my last gasped breath, the glimpse of a pale blue sky, and then my last thought as I went under:

I hope they noticed a helmet sinking . . .

The worst and scariest training sessions were called the helo-dunker. Imagine being strapped into a helicopter simulator with a co-pilot and four other crew. Once everyone is strapped in, the entire apparatus is dropped into a training tank of water from around twenty feet up. No one is allowed to move until the "aircraft" sinks down about twenty feet, where it is rotated on cables, turned over and up-ended in order to disorientate everyone. Once the movement stops, you have to count down from ten, after which all six on board have to find their way out of a specific hatch designated by the instructors just before the drop into the water. Everyone must do this wearing swim goggles that are blacked-out in order to make him completely blind. It's an interesting situation that can easily lead to panic.

In order to get out safely of course, the trick is not to panic, release your safety harness, and never lose your reference point. One hand must always be grabbing some part of the aircraft interior as you work your way out. You never release the reference point you have until your other hand reaches out and grabs a new one. So even as you float upside down, disoriented in total darkness, the one hold that you always have, gives your inner mind the reference point it needs, and by using your mind's eye, you are able to find your way to the required exit hatch.

One of my roommates had to be pulled out by rescue divers when he panicked and failed to get his harness to release. He almost drowned. The fear on his face when he was helped out of the water was real. And since he had failed, we all failed. Without hesitation, he and the rest of us were all immediately loaded up to try again. There was no time to dwell on his near-drowning experience. Instead, we were all strapped back in again—and again—and again, until we all got it right, until we all beat our fear of drowning.

"Those must have been very intense feelings," Leo-tai said. "After all, fear is a normal response to something dangerous or threatening. While many would say that fear is healthy, it is no good if fear seizes control, especially when we may have to save ourselves or save others. Fear can ruin our potential to perform."

"So, how can you stop fear from seizing control?" I asked.

"Controlling fear involves two things: a choice and a strategy. The choice is whether we truly choose to confront the fear, and then the strategy is how we go forward, having made the choice to do so. Naturally in the Navy, they made the choice for you and you were forced to confront your fears. They applied their strategy whether you guys liked it or not, and so pushed you beyond your fears."

Leo-tai looked me straight in the eyes.

"Fear can create tension, doubt, anxiety, loss of coordination, and loss of concentration. In the worst cases, fear can even begin effectively shutting down neuro-muscular connections! Someone who is afraid naturally tends to shift their focus on to what can go wrong, and when they do that, Danielsan, mistakes begin to happen—typically the very mistakes they are most fearful of making."

"I see what you're saying, how the thought of something going wrong can make it worse," I agreed.

"Fear can cause the warrior to focus on the negative. The fearful competitor can become over-cautious and decide to play it safe—instead of playing to win.

Fear can turn a competitor from someone trying to win, into someone trying not to lose. Once that confidence is gone, any advantage that the warrior may have had over his opponent begins to disappear."

"But how do you manage fear?"

Leo-tai smiled at my question. "Where is the fear? Fear happens inside your head, and thus it can be managed. A certain amount of fear energy is normal in competitive or dangerous situations. What's important is to not let it grow out of control—and to know what to do in case it does. Remember this: A champion knows that fear is only as powerful as he lets it become. Fear of something in the future—or even in the past, for that matter—can also be a tremendously powerful experience. Therefore, it is important and necessary to take back some of the power of the emotion. The Warrior/Champion does this by bringing himself back into the present moment, and the easiest way to do that, Danielsan, is to focus and watch your breathing. You must bring your breathing under control in order to ground yourself in the present."

"You mean, make a decision to focus on your breathing?"

"Exactly. That's where we start. You must focus and breathe in a controlled way. Watch your breathing. Control your breathing. Doing this has a calming effect; but more importantly, it brings you back into the present moment. Once you are back, once you have returned to the present— you (or any warrior) must then face his fear."

"Confront your fear," I suggested.

"Indeed. Ask yourself what you are so afraid of? Confront it rationally. Face your fear down. This you must do before you can set off to accomplish whatever it is that you must. Recalling times when you have been successful in the past, or successful during training, can help shut down fear. Recalling how well you typically perform, how much you love the sport, the competition, the challenge, or how well you do your job, can also prove helpful. Then, you must decide upon a strategy and move ahead embracing the challenge set before you - despite any fear."

It all sounded possible and even empowering, but I still had one question.

"How do I prevent the negative thoughts that help make me fearful?" I asked.

"Interrupt them, the instant that you notice them," he said. "Replace them—drown them out—with positive self-talk and images. You must re-direct the energy of fear and channel it into self-confidence. This is one way that you can begin to transform the energy."

He then rose. "There is only one energy prior to a confrontation or a major challenge, and the energy is telling you to get ready. If you feel the energy to be more like fear rather than self-confidence —remember that it is happening in your head. Against fear, Danielsan, you must have the spirit of attack, against fear, one can always win."

Remember: Against fear, one can always win. Confront the fear and then engage a strategy to move forward despite the fear.

Chapter 14: On Performance Choking

Leo-tai and I were discussing a national competition which we'd just watched together.

"Have you ever noticed," he mused, "how sometimes, even when an athlete's performance seems to be going really well, that it's almost as if some sort of stress takes hold of their entire game and everything starts going downhill for them?"

How interesting I thought: he's so right. Why is it that big leads and strong advantages all seem to crumble and disappear under pressure sometimes? No player is immune to it; even great champions sometimes fall victim to it. In the end, even they will admit that at one time or another, they too have "choked."

"So what causes it," I asked, "and what can be done to fight it? What about the guy in the tournament? Did he just suddenly become afraid of losing?"

"In a way, but not exactly, because a choking episode begins when a competitive situation threatens the athlete's ego," said Leo-tai. "It's a little like having a fear of failure—but choking goes beyond the fear because choking is the actual physical response that's triggered by the psychological threat to the ego. Choking is more than just having a fear of failure—fear is in your head. Choking happens when performance is actually affected by the nervousness, stress, and worries about looking bad if things go wrong. It's very different from the fear of facing a dangerous or life-threatening situation. These are subtle distinctions, but big differences."

"Yes," I admitted, "but I'm not sure that I can tell the difference."

"Perhaps that's because the physical symptoms brought on are so similar. But remember that their causes are different. Nervousness and stress in either situation will affect an athlete's breathing pattern to the point where the delivery of oxygen to the brain and muscles suffers, and he begins to feel anxiety. As an ineffective breathing pattern kicks in, his performance begins to suffer just when he needs his skills the most, just when the pressure's really on. However, choking is actually caused by an ego that's worried about looking bad, not by any real or perceived danger."

"So what could that champion have done?"

Leo-tai shook his head. "His mistake was that he let his fear of looking bad take hold and gain momentum, bringing on the nervousness and anxiety that caused the actual choking reaction. What he needed to do was to start using focused breathing, thus beginning to reduce anxiety on the spot. As one uses focused breathing, one is able to begin to relax. Oxygen fills the body, reanimating the muscles and causing anxiety to subside. Suppleness returns, bringing renewed confidence with it. Feel the relaxation as you exhale; as you begin to bring anxiety under control, things begin to get better for you."

Leo-tai switched off the TV.

"In these cases, one must use focused breathing to help bring you back into control, back into the present, and to allow yourself to feel the pressure subside . . . But Danielsan, remember: since choking springs from your ego, it's not enough to address the physical symptoms alone, although it's OK to start with them. As soon as focused breathing begins to help, you must also take control back from the ego."

"Go on," I said.

"To do this, momentarily pick a focus point in your immediate environment and fix your eyes on it as you continue your focused breathing. This will help shift the focus away from yourself and to refocus on the particular task at hand. The outside focus helps us to reduce the ego focus—which is really what is causing all the problems in the first place . . . Once an athlete really understands what

87

causes choking, he can set out to shut it down so that he can immediately begin to refocus on the challenge at hand, and keep it from getting worse. Once you see choking for what it really is, you can avoid the experience by using this strategy. Learn to leave your ego outside of your event, or it will always end up getting in the way."

Remember: Performance choking is caused by an ego that is afraid of looking bad. You must learn to leave your ego outside of your event.

Chapter 15: Cool Under Pressure

I had been several years out of the military—and I'd just been put through the mill. The Federal agents questioning me reviewed their notes, exchanged glances with each other, and then turned towards me.

"You're free to go," said the Special Agent in Charge. "That'll do."

I glanced at my watch, surprised to realize that over two hours had gone by without my noticing. During those hours, I had been grilled non-stop by all the top supervisory agents in the District Office. I supposed the reason was because I was up against a lot of strong competitors. At any rate, I rose, nodded my thanks, and headed for the door.

Just before I reached it, the lead agent called me back.

"Oh, just one more thing," he said. "I have one final question, if you don't mind?"

"Not without my lawyer," I told him, with a straight face.

They all smiled; one chuckled. (Wow, I thought: these people do have a sense of humor.)

"I've noticed that you've had some valuable training and experience as a sports mental trainer. I can't help wondering if you were using any of those mental techniques that you teach athletes during the interview today."

I smiled and looked at him.

"Absolutely," I told him. "Of course I used mental techniques today."

Later he told me how he noticed that the pressure that the panel was so good at creating, and that they had used so successfully to rattle other applicants, had appeared to have had no effect on me at all . . . And so began my career as a Special Agent.

Pressure. Intense pressure. I had known plenty of it in the military. If there's one thing that most athletes will tell me they want their mental training programs to help them with right away, it's being able to perform better under pressure.

Of course, feeling the pressure of competition is not in itself a bad thing; it can actually help to bring out the best in you. It's really how you deal with it that makes the difference. Whatever you may think, the truth is that all the pressure you feel really comes from inside yourself. Once you understand this, you can begin to free yourself to do what you are really capable of.

So, how does stress and pressure adversely affect performance?

Coordination, concentration, and judgment are all affected. Your heart beats faster, your breathing speeds up, you can't think as clearly as usual. Often, pressure creates tension that can push you to try and get through something quicker. Yet when you yield to this impulse to rush, you'll actually perform worse.

Not knowing how to handle pressure will certainly affect overall performance. This can be the undoing of any performer whether in the boardroom, on the concert stage, or while engaged in top-level sports. The first thing you have to learn is how to stay cool. This is probably the biggest single difference between a typical competitor and a mental athlete.

The mental athlete has learned how to stay calm and task-focused under pressure. He knows that staying cool is part of his success formula. So he sets out to manage the pressure—which begins by first recognizing that it's OK to feel the pressure. He doesn't deny his nerves, but he doesn't give into them either.

Here are some of the tried—and—tested techniques the mental athlete should learn to use in order to help him to stay calm and task-focused under pressure:

Learn to concentrate and use focused breathing. The athlete can bring himself back to the present moment by training himself to use his breathing to help secure control when the heat is on.

In pressure situations, make sure to let the air reach into the very bottom of your lungs. Fill every corner of your body with life-giving, life-enhancing oxygen.

Then, as you release the breath, release any tension and anxiety along with it. Notice the feeling of release—and the feeling of control. Focused breathing will help reduce the pressure and keep you grounded in the present.

An athlete can also help take the pressure off by using muscle relaxation skills. Having developed this skill through practice outside the competitive environment, the athlete equips himself with an invaluable tactic to use against the building tension and pressure that he may be feeling in a competitive environment. The ability to instantly relax muscles not only relieves tension, but also serves to calm your mind and reduce the pressures you're feeling. With a little practice, you can get really good at triggering physical relaxation quickly. Be sure to learn and practice the relaxation induction technique introduced in Chapter 7, which is extremely popular among the world's top athletes and performers.

Some athletes find that they deal best with performance pressures by using coping affirmations. The ability to talk yourself through a pressure situation is an important skill. Coping affirmations are powerful because they help you to deal with the pressure—not to pretend that the pressure doesn't exist. Many champions create and have their own personal affirmations. (I'm good, I'm fast, I'm strong, this is my time, believe, I dominate.) What they may be doesn't matter as long as they help you take the pressure off yourself. Create three quick affirmations (positive statements) you can fire off to yourself to complement the breathing and relaxation techniques mentioned above.

Another method some athletes use to deal with pressure is simply thinking about something that relaxes them. Some do this while wearing headphones listening to whatever it may be that helps them take the pressure off themselves. One athlete may be sitting in her chair at a crossover in a serious international tennis match, but she's actually no longer there. In her mind, she has transported herself somewhere else, perhaps to a tranquil mountain stream where she sits peacefully as the sun reflects in the running water. How's that for a simple approach that can make a big difference? Be sure to take the time to practice and develop this type of mental focus.

Some champions admit to using a technique from sports psychology where they allow themselves to let go of the need to achieve any particular outcome. This is all about feeling the pressure—and then warmly accepting it. Such athletes approach performances with the exhilaration of knowing that all their hard training is about to pay off and that it's time to go out and enjoy performing their sport.

They set out to compete with the feeling that they have nothing to lose. Confident that their years of solid training will take over, they let go of any remaining worries and set out to perform with uninhibited abandon. Some athletes talk about having experienced their greatest moment in sports through releasing themselves from any fear of failure.

In other words, not being focused on the outcome allowed them to become enjoyably absorbed in the process. One can sense this attitude at times when a youthful challenger "takes on" a top seed. He (or she) is almost carefree with the sense that they, at least, have nothing to lose. Some spectacular upsets have happened when a challenger has convinced himself to release the weight of his own expectations in this way. Afterwards, such athletes sometimes describe how they weren't worried about doing well, how they became completely immersed in the activity of the moment. Their chances of achieving the outcome that they desired increased dramatically when they took the pressure off themselves and let go of the need to achieve any specific outcome.

Other athletes have a ritual or pre-game routine that they like to stick with and that helps them deal with the pressure. If this is you (and it works) why mess with it?

And finally, one other approach is to recall a time when you managed a pressurized situation really well. Go back in your mind's eye and take note of exactly what you did right. What worked? What did you do? Were you still for a while before going into the match? Were you able to lose yourself in the moment? What was your self-talk like? What was going on inside your head that helped you reduce the pressure? Pinpoint it. Noticing the things that helped you deal with pressure in the past can makes it possible for you to access those techniques again. A competitor who is not feeling the pressure can easily end up defeating one who actually plays better than they do. Learning how to manage pressure can help you outperform others. If there is anything that worked for you and helped you with pressure in the past, pinpoint it, and then keep using it.

Remember: Pressure is mental. Learn to view performance pressure as a challenge that can be managed by using mental techniques and pre-game routines.

Chapter 16: The Internal Critic

As I transitioned more and more into coaching, Leo-tai and I often spoke by phone. In those days he enjoyed hearing about the work that I was doing at a large university as the Mental Edge Trainer for the athletes on the various teams.

One day I explained to him how, after the wrestling competitions, the head coach and I would review all the tapes. Then how (one by one) each wrestler was brought in to sit down and watch his tape with us. Mostly the head coach would make suggestions regarding technique or strategy. A few days later I would review some of the tapes again with the guys who hadn't done so well. But this time I asked the athletes to recall what their self-talk was during the toughest parts of the match.

"Very good," said Leo-tai. "You found something in common?"

"We certainly did," I said. "The one thing we found that they all had in common was that they all had negative self-talk going on when things were going really badly. By watching themselves on tape, they were able to remember exactly what they were thinking at the time. And in every case of poor performance, when things were going really badly, the self-talk going through their heads was terrible. Their own internal dialogue was setting them up to perform worse and worse. At the precise instances when they needed all their resolve in order to be able to turn things around, their self-talk was busy tearing them down."

"Interesting," Leo-tai said quietly.

"So we'd play the tape again, only this time the exercise was to have the athletes verbalize positive self-talk as things got bad. I'd say, 'This time, let me hear the positive self-talk of a champion who might be having a tough time during the match but who absolutely refuses to talk himself down.' Then, as we'd watch, they'd adjust their self-talk. That exercise really opened their eyes. They learned that— especially when things are tough—it's most important to listen only for the positive self-talk of a champion who is focused on working his way through adversity."

At this point Leo-tai offered up an observation.

"Very good Danielsan, you taught them to shut down the Internal Critic. You taught them to always listen for the self-talk that sounds more like a positive coach rather than a negative critic. You helped them understand that if there is any self-talk going on it must be positive, encouraging, and empowering. This is key because just like thoughts create emotions that affect the way we feel, so can self-talk affect the way we feel, and the way we feel affects the way that we perform. Always remind them Danielsan, the Warrior/Champion shuts down the Internal Critic because he understands that he must."

Remember: Especially when things are at their worst, your self-talk must be positive, encouraging, and empowering. Shut down the Internal Critic.

Chapter 17: Too Intense

Sometimes in competitive situations an athlete can actually get too energized before the start of competition, thus sabotaging his own performance. You see it a lot in grappling tournaments where (due to sheer over-enthusiasm) some amateur athletes rev up their engines to fever pitch before even stepping out on to the mat. What they fail to understand is that coming in too high on the performance curve will actually end up hurting their performance.

Years ago, this kept happening to an athlete that I was helping to train. No matter how much he visualized calmness, coolness and control, no sooner did the day of the competition dawn than he was crackling with anticipation and incapable of even eating for sheer excitement. The result was that, although he tended to start out powerfully, he was too energized, and it hurt his performance. His competitors soon had him on the defensive. This was very frustrating for him, until he learned through practice how to adjust the level of intensity at which he entered into competition. By learning to adjust his intensity down by just a notch or two as he entered competition, the athlete began to win more often.

A good mental athlete learns early on at what level of intensity he plays his best game. On a scale of one to ten (with ten being at the most intense level) most top athletes report that they perform best at around levels seven or eight. Occasionally, of course, they may need to call on their full intensity and "raise their game" to nine or ten. But they still know that this is not the ideal level of intensity at which to enter a competition.

By getting to know at what level of intensity he should begin, the mental athlete has a big advantage. He is helping to create the conditions needed in order for him to perform really well. He manages his intensity so it doesn't interfere with his best game. It's a simple concept that can make a vital difference—yet so few amateurs are aware of it. You can't rev yourself up to a level ten each time and expect to consistently perform at your best. Your neuro-muscular connections are able to deliver better physical technique as you learn to throttle back your level of intensity.

Self-analysis and advice from people you trust will help you to pinpoint precisely at what level of intensity you generally find your best game. Try to make a note of what pre-game routine worked to help get you to the exact level where you are most effective, and then practice arriving at your ideal intensity level at exactly the right moment. Learn to manage all that valuable intensity.

Remember: You have to learn to control yourself before standing a chance of controlling your game. Getting your intensity revved up too powerfully prior to competition will actually hurt your performance.

Chapter 18: Your Dream

At certain times in my life I've looked around and found myself having (temporarily) achieved my goals. Looking back on all the hardships, the obstacles, the challenges, and even some of the negative people who'd done their best to try to keep me down, somehow I still did what I intended to do, and got myself where I wanted to be.

So, what is it that drives us to try again and again, to keep going, to keep taking just one more step even when nothing seems to be working for us?

A dream, that's what.

Think about it. Without a dream, without a vision, how can you know where you hope to get? Without a dream one is only drifting.

So, what's your dream? If it's important to you, then it's worth chasing. Any champion will tell you that a big part of life involves reaching for your dreams. It's what helps you move forward.

Remember what Walt Disney called Imagineering? Use it, as you set out to create your vision. Let Imagineering help you build the confidence that you can get to your dream; allow yourself to be moved by the power of your dreams. Never let anyone or anything shove you off track or break you down once you've set your course towards achieving something.

A friend of mine dreamed of becoming a lawyer. Despite the fact that nobody in his entire extended family had even been to college before, his immediate goal was to get to the University of Chicago. And, once he was there, his immediate goal was to graduate top of his class. Once he'd done that, he adjusted his dream again: to passing the Illinois bar exam. And once he'd done that, to becoming one of Chicago's top lawyers. Even once he'd succeeded in that goal, he wasn't finished dreaming. He then dreamed that he could, through the position he'd worked so hard all his life to attain, make life better for the underprivileged kids in the area where he'd grown up. That's what I call positive dreaming.

So, where do you see yourself next? What's your vision of your future? One thing's for sure, if you ever hope to achieve it, you need to see it and feel it, vividly, in your mind's eye, and not just occasionally. Learn to often reinforce your vision of where you hope to be in a few years time—and then work towards achieving it.

It's not only dreaming, of course, but also believing and taking action. You've got to take specific steps to get you where you want to be. Soon you'll learn some simple goal setting ideas that can help you transform your dreams into reality. They're the same ideas that many top performers use in order to help them make steady progress, but for now, I want you to get a clear vision of what it is that you want to achieve for yourself.

Think about what you want to become, how you want things to be. For a little while, you need to do some Imagineering. Close your eyes and see yourself and everything around you the way you want it to be. Imagine it, feel it, see it clearly, see it vividly. Let your spirit soar.

Decide: What's your dream? Figure it out. That's your assignment.

Chapter 19: On Goals

Warrior/Champions set out to turn their dreams into reality by taking action through goal setting. Often, personal growth and peak performance are directly related to how well an athlete has mastered goal-setting skills. Mental athletes are goal-oriented. They have vision.

When an athlete complains of lacking motivation, you can be sure that it's almost always caused by goals that fail to inspire him to action. Goals serve to keep you on target. They increase the desire to achieve. Goals increase your self-confidence as you experience measurable improvement. With proper goal setting, the quality of practice sessions automatically improves. Goals enhance performance, and help create achievements.

While setting your own, private goals, be sure that they are both challenging and realistic. Slightly out-of-reach goals are best: inspiring hard work, yet still attainable with dedicated effort. Goals need to be set neither too high, nor too easy and low—which would defeat their very purpose. Goals should be written down and reviewed frequently. Goals should come in the forms of daily goals, monthly goals and annual goals, and remember that what you are striving for is progress rather than perfection. Believe me, as you begin to focus on meaningful, specific goals, the power of your hidden reserves will be unleashed and good things will begin to happen.

I well remember when I came to meet Leo-tai with "Goals 1 to 25" neatly transcribed which I proudly showed him.

Leo-tai stroked his chin.

"Hmmm," is all he said and I was instantly on the defensive. (Hmmm with Leo-tai never meant, "Well done.")

"What do you mean?" I demanded. "Aren't those good goals? If I achieve those rankings, I'd be one of the top kick-boxers on the scene."

Leo-tai walked into his tiny, immaculate little kitchen, and returned with two green teas. "My friend," he asked, "are these your goals or did you have help in deciding upon them?"

I wondered how that might be bad.

"Listen, Danielsan. Goals are most meaningful when they are what you truly want for yourself, not what others want for you."

"OK, but I do want these goals," I objected, a little annoyed.

"Secondly," he said, paying no attention at all, "what's this you have written here, 'Don't lose in the early rounds at nationals.' "

"What's wrong with that?"

Leo-tai shook his head.

"How many times must I remind you that you must make sure to state your goals in a way that emphasizes what you want to happen, not what you want to avoid. This 'don't lose in the early rounds' is not a goal at all, it's fearful."

I looked at the 25 things I'd written down more carefully now. Around a quarter of them were negative-orientated. I scrunched the paper into a ball and having let the paper fly; I made a perfect goal, straight into the waste-basket.

"So what am I supposed to do then?"

Leo-tai beamed.

"There is nothing wrong with your goals, but you must lay them out thoughtfully. Ask yourself what you want to accomplish over the next two or three years. Make these your long-term goals. Give them a completion date."

"Right. And then?"

"Then think of at least three things that you want to achieve within the next year. Make these your short-term goals.

Give them a completion date," he told me.

"And then what?" I asked him.

"Then decide what it is that you can do every month to help you accomplish your short-term goals," he said. "Write these down. These are your monthly goals. Give them a completion date too."

"Set daily goals, that help you achieve monthly goals, that help you achieve your short-term goals, that in turn help you achieve your long-term goals. When your goals fit together this way and you set off to accomplish them, you make progress. But first you must make sure it's your dream and not anybody else's dream—this is the way forward. Any more tea?" he asked.

"No, thanks," I said. I was busy thinking about what he had given me. With this framework it all seemed comparatively simple. I found myself consumed with the desire to start listing my goals over again, more patiently, more logical, more perfectly.

"Do it now," Leo-tai urged me. "Use the guidelines and the system of goal setting I just described for you. I challenge you to create your plan. Start right now and point yourself in the right direction by taking the steps necessary to begin to accomplish your goals and dreams."

Leo-tai poured himself more tea.

"Think deeply. Everything you need is inside of you, inside

your very dreams. Goals represent your dreams along a timeline, showing you the steps needed to achieve your success. Remember that every journey is taken step by step. So start thinking. Be creative, take risks, try things, and most importantly, set your goals before you—and believe in your ability to accomplish them. If I were you, I would start right now."

For the next few days, I was busy thinking and dreaming. I took his lesson seriously. I have never regretted having done so.

Remember: Setting goals is critical because they help you achieve. They represent your dreams along a timeline and help you to progress.

Chapter 20: Do the Work

Once, after having knocked out his opponent during a professional Mixed Martial Arts event, Renzo Gracie was interviewed by a commentator who suggested that Renzo had only won because he'd been lucky. Without missing a beat, and with a shrewd smile on his face, Renzo famously replied, "Well, the harder I work, the luckier I get!"

What a champion—and what a true champion's response!

With very few exceptions, the truth is that the best athletes usually turn out to be the ones who work the hardest. While most athletes will tell you that they want to win, very few of those talented enough to make it to the top are willing to put in the hard work and dedication that becoming a champion demands. As a coach it's easy for me to spot the athlete determined enough to be willing to pay the price. For a start, it shows in the effort and consistency put forth during practice. Secondly, the best athletes love the process of doing what it takes to become the best they can be. There's a measurable difference in their level of commitment and confidence over most athletes because they actually enjoy working hard at getting better.

Listen to what legendary football coach Vince Lombardi once wrote about this type of commitment: "A man can be as great as he wants to be, if you believe in yourself and have the courage, the determination, the dedication, the competitive drive, and if you are willing to sacrifice the little things in life and pay the price for the things that are worthwhile, anything can be done. Once a man has made a commitment, he puts the greatest strength in the world behind him, this thing we call heart power. Once a man has made this commitment, nothing will stop him short of success. The harder you work the harder it is to surrender."

Yet in spite of this, quite often an athlete with astonishing levels of God-given talent chooses to cruise along without putting much effort into improving himself. He gets comfortable and rather than working hard to take his talent onto another level, he doesn't put in the work required. Eventually, many harder-working athletes will surpass such athletes. So don't be discouraged if you're not exactly what a coach would consider a huge talent. Hard work, effort and enthusiasm will still bring you good results as long as you stay the course. And if you happen to be extremely talented, just remember that such talent can be either a blessing or a curse. Talent is no blessing if you let yourself stagnate because playing well comes relatively easily to you. The mental athlete knows that in order to excel one can't just do enough to get by.

After one of my young students won a national

championship, I asked him if it felt good to see all his hard work finally pay off. He admitted that it felt pretty good, that he was really happy.

"So what are your plans now Mr. National Champ?" I teased him. "Are you going to take a break?"

"No way," he said. "Now every kid wants to beat me, I have to work even harder now if I'm going to stay champion."

Smart twelve-year-old. He'd already realized that he was going to have to work harder than ever in order to maintain his high level of success. Yet I could tell by the gleam in his eye that he was excited about the prospect.

The truth is that real champions want to do the work. They are willing to do not only whatever it takes to get to the top, but also whatever it takes to stay at the top. True champions are willing to pay the price in order to improve.

Think about what Renzo Gracie told that commentator, "The harder I work, the luckier I get!"

So . . . how determined are you to make your own luck happen?

Remember: Once you really make the commitment to work hard at becoming a champion, something powerful is set in motion—heart power.

Chapter 21: Getting There

Many times, after working with a professional fighter or an advanced grappler, they thank me for having shown them something they claim never to have been taught before. That makes me feel great, and one reason for my gratification is because they trust me enough to admit that (even as great competitors) they don't know it all. That's a true champion, in a nutshell. A true champion always recognizes that, if you're open to learning something today, it can make you an even greater champion tomorrow.

There's never a stage in our careers when we've learned so much that there's nothing left to learn. And this is even truer once you realize that, in almost every case, champions are made, not born.

A true champion accepts that (as great as he or she may currently be) it's not what they know that's important; it's what they can still learn that makes the biggest difference. They know that in order to reach their highest possible level they have to strive for constant and daily improvement. And they know that the fastest way to improve is to work, not on their strengths, but on their weaknesses.

Therefore, in order to improve, the mental athlete must be resolutely clear on exactly what his strengths and weaknesses are. Then (and this is the important part) he or she must determine to change weaknesses into strengths.

Take the true example of a young and gifted tennis player with a devastating serve and a wonderful forehand, but a rather weak backhand, always slicing it back to her opponent. Once while she was working with her coach, belting back excellent forehand after forehand, she overheard someone say that her forehand was so reliable already that she was crazy not to concentrate on her backhand. For the next couple of weeks she told her coach she wanted to concentrate entirely upon upgrading her backhand. Shortly thereafter, she achieved one of her biggest career wins ever, toppling the world's top-ranked player in the second round of an international tournament! She had changed a weakness into one of her strengths.

Your game plan ought to be the same: pinpoint your weaknesses and set out to work extra hard on them. While it's true that it's important to work on all aspects of your game, a champion knows that a good opponent will find and exploit any weaknesses; therefore he develops an action plan to target and improve on all the things that he knows are not his strongest points.

So . . . what don't you do quite so well? And do you have an action plan to change it? Look at your game like a champion. Set out to make yourself better than ever by pinpointing what to improve! And don't put it off because some parts of your game are already working. Adapting to good advice that comes your way, and working hard to change your weaknesses into strengths, will help take your entire game to another level.

So commit yourself, get an action plan in place and make it a point to improve by setting out to transform your weaknesses into strengths.

Remember: Successful people have the self-discipline to do the things that have to be done, whether they enjoy them or not.

Chapter 22: Changing Your Mental State

Changing your state. What's that mean, exactly?

Remember my unbeliever from Chapter One? What kind of state was he in before he turned it around? If you recall, he was in a very disempowered state when he sought me out. He was nervous, fearful, anxious, tense, and entirely lacking self-confidence. In short, there was no way that he could do well in competition unless he changed his state.

So, what did he do in those few minutes that made all the difference?

Recall that, with little coaching, he changed his state from being totally fearful and disempowered to being totally confident and prepared for competition. He literally became an unchained force of dominance. And he did it so quickly!

I promised that I would teach you how to do what he did, so here we go. With everything you've learned so far, I know you are ready. Here's what you need to understand, and here's exactly how to go about doing it for yourself.

Thoughts create the emotions and feelings that are the cause of your state. Whatever state that may be, your own thoughts put you there. So, whenever you find yourself in a disempowered state remember this: you can alter your thoughts and your state by focusing on three different critical elements.

The First Critical Element: Self-Talk. Ask yourself: What would the self-talk of a champion sound like as he prepared for competition?

I took my unbeliever aside and I asked him a simple question, "If you were a great champion with tons of experience at this level, and if you had an incredible record, and if you were at the top of your game where no one could touch you, what would your self-talk sound like as you prepared to go into this match?"

My unbeliever looked at me, "I don't know, coach."

"Well, how about things like: I'm strong, I'm fast, I dominate. I control the match, I never give in, I never give up. I'm powerful, I beat my opponent, I'm an unchained lethal gladiator, I conquer. I'm an unstoppable champion, a force of fury, my opponent submits. Or how about these? I'm ready, I take charge, I keep going, I don't let up, I win, I'm tougher, I'm stronger, I'm better, I stop my opponent.

Get the idea?" I asked.

"Yep," he said.

"Good. Then that's what I want. Pretend you're an actor. Start being that champion. Start hearing the self-talk of that champion," I told him. "I want you to pretend and feel that you are this champion I just described. I want you to start firing off, inside your head, the same self-talk that this champion would have going through his head as he gets ready for a match. Start now," I told him looking at my watch. "We don't have much time."

I shut up and watched him as he immersed himself in his task. At this point Jeremy began firing off the self-talk of a champion in his head. He stayed nearby as he walked around, pacing, putting all his focus and his entire being into the exercise.

After about a minute I got his attention again. "Good, very good," I said, "now we are going to add something to it."

The Second Critical Element: The way that you carry your body. Ask yourself: How would this champion's body be moving as he prepared for battle?

"Jeremy," I said, "start moving your body around as this champion that is preparing for competition."

He was listening hard. I continued, "Keep on seeing yourself as this champion, keep the self-talk going, and at the same time I want you to now start moving your body around as if you were this champion getting ready to beat your opponent down. How would you be moving your body? How would you, as this champion, carry yourself as you prepared for the match? Show me. Starting right now," I added, "you get another minute."

Jeremy sprang into action. Before my eyes he started moving his body around like a champion warming up, getting ready to do battle, pacing, and practicing on an imaginary opponent, full of energy, like a caged gladiator waiting to be released. And, as I watched, I began to have hope. Jeremy's body motions became like those of a champion annihilator.

At the same time, as he moved his body around like this champion annihilator, Jeremy kept firing off the self-talk of this champion in his head.

Now we had the self-talk of a champion going, and the body movements of a champion preparing for battle going on. I let him do his work. I didn't disturb him for another minute or so.

The Third Critical Element: Breathing. Watching Jeremy's imagination, self-talk, and body motions begin to turn things around for him, I threw in the third element. "Jeremy," I asked, "how would this champion be breathing right now as he prepared for battle? Keep the self-talk going, keep moving your body around as this champion, and now, I want you to add the breathing of a champion getting ready to do battle."

Without missing a beat, Jeremy adjusted his breathing. Now he had all three critical elements going. Breathing, movement, and self-talk. Jeremy was in a different world.

At the end of those few minutes, Jeremy had changed his state completely. When he walked on to that mat, he was ready mentally and physically, and he was therefore able to deliver one of his best performances ever. By bringing all three critical elements together in this way, Jeremy, my unbeliever, got out of his own way, he changed his state, he let his training take over, and he competed like a true champion.

That's how he did it, and that's how you can do it too.

As part of your pre-competition routine . . .

Ask yourself: What would the self-talk of a champion be like as he prepared for competition?

How would that champion be moving his body around as he prepared?

And how would that champion be breathing as he prepared to enter the competition and face his opponent?

Then do it. Bring it all together for several minutes prior to your time, and allow yourself to enter into this totally prepared and empowered state before you compete. Get out of your own way. Let your training take over.

Remember: Use all three critical elements and bring them together in order to change your state completely—The Self-talk of a Champion preparing to do battle, the Body Movements of a Champion preparing to do battle, and the Breathing of a Champion preparing to do battle. Then, allow yourself to become that Champion as you enter your competition.

Chapter 23: The Present

I was finishing my studies at the university. One day Leo-tai called me and said that he wanted to come out to visit and see where I was in the Black Hills. He said he also wanted to see where Rocky Raccoon from the old Beatles' song used to run around.

Then he started right into it . . .

"Now somewhere in the Black Mountain Hills of Dakota, lived a young boy named Rocky Raccoon, and one day his woman run off with another guy, hit young Rocky in the eye . . ."

Leo-tai sung it over the phone. It was funny; he really had it down.

So, as so often happened, Leo-tai ended up doing what he wanted to do. Now, here was Leo-tai, smack in the Black Hills, visiting me. He was very excited to be so near the home of Rocky Raccoon.

And, when I told him that I figured Rocky Raccoon ran around in Deadwood: "Then we'll have to go up there for sure," he said.

We were in a beautiful part of the Black Hills where I rented a place at the mouth of Spearfish Canyon while I finished school. There I took Leo-tai on a short hike up a trail ending high above the canyon.

The stunning view took Leo-tai by surprise.

"Danielsan," he said with amazement, "this is very good."

"Incredible, isn't it?"

"This is very good indeed!" he said with his widest smile.

I showed him where to sit in order to enjoy one of the best places in the world from which to watch a sunset. I pulled out two Gatorades and my journal in order to jot down his thoughts as we watched what we later agreed was one of the most beautiful sunsets we'd ever seen.

Leo-tai's lessons were always concise and to the point. He never went too fast, he kept it simple.

"To be totally in the *Present*, Danielsan . . . that is the key. To learn how to be there throughout the competition, that is your goal. To consistently play in the Present moment, where mind and body are as one, where training takes over, where no thoughts interfere. This is Warrior knowledge, Danielsan, it is something that has been taught for centuries.

You are being shown an established way to get there."

Leo-tai's eyes were far over the horizon. He continued, "By understanding and practicing the Art one learns how to create the internal environment that invites in the quiet mind during competition. The quiet mind is a warrior skill. In the Present, everything comes together and performance is flawless and automatic. Inside, the Warrior/Champion has no thought, no cluttered mind; instead he is an unstoppable champion totally absorbed in the action before him."

As I listened I remembered having recently watched Pete Sampras being asked in an interview what he was thinking about during a crucial moment in a tennis match. His answer was fascinating, proving his total immersion in the moment. "Nothing," he replied. "I was thinking about nothing."

"A true champion," said Leo-tai, "learns how to feel no pressure, because pressure is created by anxiety, and anxiety can only exist if one allows one's thoughts to wander away from the Present to some uncertainty in the future or to some remembered failure of the past . . . There is power in the Present moment, Danielsan: hold on to it."

"The two skills the Warrior/Champion must possess to help him reach his maximum potential are the ability to recognize when his mind is not focused on the Present, and the ability to bring it back into the Present. When your mind is racing, help bring it back by focusing on your breathing. This will help you to reach that place where we have a sure sense that we can do what we know we need to do, and that we can do it without having to try too hard, a place from where technique flows freely and accurately, a place from which right action springs forth."

"You mean the quiet mind," I said.

"Exactly, and the Present moment is where the quiet mind exists. There's no worry, no judging, no fearing, no hoping; the mind is totally in the here and *Now* throughout the event. You must practice leaving all the mental clutter, all the personal situations, all the distractions that fill up your head, outside of the arena. While it's crucial to have learned from the past, there is also a time to leave the past behind you. And while it's important to prepare for the future, to be in the Present requires that it too, must be discarded at some level."

Leo-tai looked at me carefully to make sure that I understood his point.

"*Now* is the time in which you perform, and the Present is the only place that *Now* exists. Practice quieting the mind, and bringing it to the Present. Learn to be still, learn to find the Present, in order to be able to perform at your highest level—do you understand?"

"I think so," I told him.

125

"Then you must practice more, Danielsan, so that you may *know* so."

Once again, Leo-tai had helped me to better understand his Warrior Art.

Remember: "To be totally in the *Present*, that is the key."

Chapter 24: Prepare to Win

I had been training with Leo-tai for many years. Now I had been accepted into the Navy flight program, and we both knew that it might be a long time before I'd be back.

"You must prepare to win," Leo-tai told me as we finished my knife-fighting lesson that night. "A champion always prepares to win."

He knew that I was listening.

"Always use mental rehearsal and imagery as you've been taught," he told me. "It builds confidence. Confidence comes from knowing you are prepared both physically *and* mentally. Confidence helps you know what to do automatically even when you're not sure. It helps immensely. Be sure to visualize."

Leo-tai began putting away the training knives that we had been using.

"You must trust yourself, Danielsan. There must be no lack

of commitment in your mind. Eliminate doubt. There's no room for it. Have confidence and trust yourself as you prepare to win . . . Always take your training sessions seriously. Always concentrate. Remember: you're creating neuro-muscular connections that are going to take over when you learn how to get out of your own way. The better you concentrate during training, the more you'll be able to trust yourself when you must fully perform."

Leo-tai continued: "Remember that mental training helps the warrior develop the ability to set the analytical mind aside long enough so that his training can take over and he can fight by instinct. When this happens you're confident, relaxed, determined. Everything flows. You experience peak performance. It's a reward for having prepared well. Remember, and never forget,—you can never force peak performance. You must prepare correctly in an effort to allow it to occur. You now understand how to go about creating the *Ideal Mental Climate* from which it springs forth."

I followed him towards the door of the studio as I finished putting on my watch cap and coat. Everything he was telling me made perfect sense.

"It's a matter of learning how to leave your conscious mind out of it," he reminded me, "and letting your training take over. And don't forget that sometimes improvement means letting go of old ways, Danielsan. So remain open to learning, and rest assured that it will take courage to achieve your goals and reach your full potential. Get ready to work

128

hard."

As I stepped outside, I got the feeling that he wasn't quite ready to let me go—I wondered later if perhaps he was remembering my brother at that moment.

He looked at me. "The most important thing is how a champion prepares for battle. You must find the warrior within. You must do battle with all your heart in order to have no regrets as you leave the contest behind. A champion always prepares to win. Remember to act like a champion in order to become a champion."

"I will," I assured him as we shook hands. He knew how grateful I was for everything.

He smiled, "You did well today."

And with that, Leo-tai brought my lesson to an end.

It would be a long time before I would see Leo-tai again. First would come Grenada, then Panama, and finally the Middle East.

Remember: A champion always prepares to win.

Chapter 25: Walk On

As we took a long walk on the coastline near his home, I caught myself reflecting on how all the years seemed to have passed by so quickly ever since that last lesson so many years ago. Leo-tai still had that same effortless stride that he'd made me keep up with so many times before . . . We walked a long time in companionable silence, surrounded by seagulls, wind, and waves.

When we finally stopped Leo-tai sat himself up on a comfortable-looking rock and I leaned up against an even bigger one. He crinkled up his eyes as he looked out to sea and I noticed for the first time that he looked tired. (How old was Leo-tai? I wondered; I'd never even asked.)

"Look at the waves," he murmured. "Endlessly renewing themselves, endlessly feeding into each other. There's no end to them. No, just the renewal and withdrawal, over and over again."

A seagull circled over the rocks.

"It is the cycle of the earth," said Leo-tai. "We're here, we're gone. We are born and we die. The world keeps turning, but too slowly for our understanding."

"I hope you're not intending to die any day soon," I joked, a bit uneasily.

"Who knows? So much is not given to us to know. But, even if this should happen, Danielsan, it is not the end. It is only the beginning of something else, something different. This is why I never say good-bye."

I was startled to realize that this was true. In all the years I'd known Leo-tai, he'd always just drifted off, or shut the door with a smile. I couldn't ever remember his saying, "Goodbye."

Something about his tone made me glance at him again, was this the goodbye he never actually said? Was he going where someone else needed him more? It had been years since we had trained together steadily, but he always seemed to be there, the voice on the end of a telephone, the letter from some place I'd never been, a presence by my shoulder, his teachings now always a part of me.

"Now," he said, once he was settled, "tell me why you are sad."

"Sad? I don't think I'd call it being sad," I said. "Perhaps feeling a little lost—somewhat incomplete . . . yes—but not sad."

So much had changed. The military had put me in hot spots all over the world. I had seen enough. I was done with it. I had managed to walk away—unlike some of my friends, and life had dealt some devastating blows. I sensed that he could tell that I wasn't kidding, that I was really disillusioned with everything . . . Yet he at least was still the same, still watching me with that old, considering look in his eyes.

"You've become disillusioned," he said.

"That's an understatement," I replied.

"There came a point when it was clear to you that where you were no longer inspired you—and you realized that if you stood still, then that's where you would stay. What's wrong with choosing to not stand still? Congratulations. Some people live their whole lives in chains without realizing that they always held the key."

He looked at me and gently shook his head.

"Danielsan, who knows what awaits you, but never mind the uncertainty that occupies your thinking right now. Understand this. Life doesn't always go the way we want it to go. You dream your dreams, you work your goals, and still, life may not go as you have planned. But think about it, where would we be if we had not chosen a path, if we had put forth no effort into achieving a plan? In those cases I would say that one had no direction at all, and there is nothing good about that."

"Well, that's exactly how I feel right now," I told my old friend. "No direction at all."

"Maybe you feel that way, Danielsan, but I don't see it that way. If someone sets themselves free—from whatever; if someone picks themselves up after life hits them with a sucker punch, that is some direction, at least—wouldn't you agree? Picking yourself up or setting yourself free is direction. It is part of achieving something."

I watched as the sun drooped down beyond the horizon ahead of us.

"Please Leo-tai, can you just help me see your point?"

"I can. My point is that even though we may not understand it, sometimes life will put us on a new path, one that we would have never asked for, that we have never dreamed of, or ever imagined, . . . And after all, isn't that what's really happening to you?"

"Instead of over-analyzing and doubting the direction your life has taken, why not simply accept the fact that there is a new path that has been set before you right now? Stop the internal self-doubt. It only causes confusion. The fact is that whatever was—is no more. It's gone. It's in the past. And whatever is—well, isn't that what really matters?"

I was listening—as I watched the waves and the seagulls.

"The past is gone my friend. You can look back on it but it's only a reflection. The future lies ahead . . . but it's a future that has not yet been realized. So in reality, today is all we have. And today is here. Why don't you just start walking on your new path, one step at a time? Conjure up some new dreams, cast them out to the universe, keep your head up, have faith, and discover what lies ahead. Life itself has put you on this path. Just trust what is and be with it."

Leo-tai continued.

"I believe that anyone who does this, Danielsan, soon finds the new path taking them in a most natural and comfortable direction. Embrace the new adventure; walk into it with strong self-belief and before long—I suspect—you will find the new direction rewarding, and amazing beyond anything that you could have ever imagined . . . Follow the path set before you; follow your destiny. The universe does not make mistakes; everyone is exactly where they need to be. You must remember this whenever it seems that the pattern of your life has lost its firmness of purpose. Always remember—you are exactly where you need to be, and then —" Leo-tai paused.

"And then what?" I asked him.

"And then my friend . . . you must walk on. You must simply—*walk on.*"

I let his words sink in. As the sun hazed into the sea, I remembered so many other sunset lessons over the years. Perhaps Leo-tai was remembering too, for he suddenly said, "From amongst all our lessons, what one most important thing do you think I would always want you to remember? If there was just one, what do you think it might be?"

So many things. I thought. I recalled the fight with the raccoons, the many mistakes I'd made, all the times he'd picked me up off of the floor, dusted me off, and started me over again. I thought hard. Learning to never give in, not allowing negativity, self-discipline, staying in the present, control of anger, control of fear, Imagineering, to believe in my dreams.

And then I remembered: "Self-belief is what gets everything going."

"Self-Belief," I told him. Our eyes met and he glowed back at me.

"Very good, Danielsan, you worried me sometimes, but not anymore," he told me. "Now, you don't worry me anymore."

"Really?" I said.

"Well, come to think of it—no, not really, I take it back."

"Too late, I already heard you say it," I joked.

"So?"

"So that's it, if I heard you say it, then it must be true, and you can't take it back . . . Besides, I've got to get going and meet up with some people. It's time for me to say goodbye."

He looked at me.

"Oh Danielsan, it's never goodbye my friend," Leo-tai reproved me, shaking his head, smiling as if he were still worried about me. "It's never goodbye," he told me as I watched him turn away—still smiling—and start his walk back along the surf.

As he slipped away, I watched him go. I let him go, a small figure, disappearing into the distance. I wondered if this might be the last time I would ever see my old friend—did he know it?—Today, I still wonder—but back then, I let him go.

And I reflected.

Once more and somehow—he had done it. What he told me, his insight that day, made sense. His lesson helped me.

And then, as he'd wanted me to . . .

And like we all must do, at one time or another . . .

We walk on.